SPREADSHEET MODELING
FUNDAMENTALS OF INVESTMENTS

01-02 Edition to accompany Alexander, Sharpe, and Bailey

CRAIG W. HOLDEN

Richard G. Brinkman Faculty Fellow and Associate Professor
Kelley School of Business
Indiana University

Prentice Hall, Upper Saddle River, New Jersey 07458

Editor in Chief: PJ Boardman
Acquisitions Editor: Maureen Riopelle
Managing Editor: Gladys Soto
Assistant Editor: Cheryl Clayton
Media Project Manager: Bill Minick
Marketing Manager: Josh McClary
Editorial Assistant: Melanie Olsen
Cover Designer: Steve Frim
 Manager, Print Production: Christy Mahon
Production Editor: Carol Zaino
Formatting: Progressive
Manufacturer: Banta Book Group

ISBN 0-13-033667-X

To Kathryn, you're the inspiration,
and to Diana and Jimmy, with joy and pride.
Craig

ABOUT THE AUTHOR

CRAIG W. HOLDEN

 Craig Holden is the Richard G. Brinkman Faculty Fellow and Associate Professor of Finance at the Kelley School of Business at Indiana University. His M.B.A. and Ph.D. are from the Anderson School at UCLA. He is the winner of multiple schoolwide teaching awards and multiple schoolwide research awards. He has written a book/CD series on **Spreadsheet Modeling** in finance, which is published by Prentice Hall. His research on security trading and market making ("market microstructure") has been published in leading academic journals. He has chaired nine dissertations, served on the program committee of the *Western Finance Association* for three years, and served as an associate editor of the *Journal of Financial Markets* for four years. He has chaired a department committee for seven years and chaired various schoolwide committees for six years. He has lead several major curriculum innovations in the finance department. For more details, Craig's home page is at **www.kelley.iu.edu/cholden**.

CONTENTS

PART 3 OPTIONS / FUTURES / DERIVATIVES   86

Preface

For nearly 20 years, since the emergence of PCs, Lotus 1-2-3, and Microsoft Excel in the 1980's, spreadsheet models have been the dominant vehicles for finance professionals in the business world to implement their financial knowledge. Yet even today, most Fundamentals of Investments textbooks rely on calculators as the primary tool and have little (if any) coverage of how to build spreadsheet models. This book fills that gap. It teaches students how to build financial models in Excel. It provides step-by-step instructions so that students can build models themselves (active learning), rather than handing students canned "templates" (passive learning). It progresses from simple examples to practical, real-world applications. It spans nearly all quantitative models in the fundamentals of investments.

Why I Wrote This Book

My goal is simply to *change finance education from being calculator based to being spreadsheet modeling based*. This change will better prepare students for the 21ˢᵗ century business world. This change will increase student satisfaction in the classroom by allowing more practical, real-world applications and by enabling a more hands-on, active learning approach.

There are many features which distinguish this book from anything else on the market:

- **Teach By Example.** I believe that the best way to learn spreadsheet modeling is by working through examples and completing a lot of problems. This book fully develops this hands-on, active learning approach. Active learning is a well-established way to increase student learning and student satisfaction with the course / instructor. When students build financial models themselves, they really "get it." As I tell my students, "If you build it, you will learn."

- **Supplement For All Popular Fundamentals of Investments Textbooks.** This book is a supplement to be combined with a primary textbook. This means that you can keep using whatever textbook you like best. You don't have to switch. It also means that you can take an incremental approach to incorporating spreadsheet modeling. You can start modestly and build up from there. Alternative notation versions are available that match the notation of all popular fundamentals of investments textbooks.

- **Plain Vanilla Excel.** Other books on the market emphasize teaching students programming using Visual Basic for Applications (VBA) or using macros. By contrast, this book does everything in plain vanilla Excel. Although programming is liked by a minority of students, it is seriously disliked by the majority. Plain vanilla Excel has the advantage of being a very intuitive, user-friendly environment that is accessible to all. It is fully capable of handling a wide range of applications, including quite sophisticated ones. Further, your students already know the basics of Excel and nothing more is assumed. Students are assumed to be able to enter formulas in a cell and to copy formulas from one cell to another. All other features of Excel (graphing, built-in functions, Solver, etc.) are explained as they are used.

- **Build From Simple Examples To Practical, Real-World Applications.** The general approach is to start with a simple example and build up to a practical, real-world application. In many chapters, the previous spreadsheet model is carried forward to the next more complex model. For example, the chapter on binomial option pricing carries forward spreadsheet models as follows: (a.) single-period model with replicating portfolio, (b.) eight-period model with replicating portfolio, (c.) eight-period model with risk-neutral probabilities, (d.) full-scale, fifty-period model with volatilities estimated from real returns data. Whenever possible, this book builds up to full-scale, practical applications using real data. Students are excited to learn practical applications that they can actually use in their future jobs. Employers are excited to hire students with spreadsheet modeling skills, who can be more productive faster.

- **A Change In Content Too.** Spreadsheet modeling is not merely a new medium, but an opportunity to cover some unique content items which require computer support to be feasible. For example, the full-scale, real data spreadsheet model in Portfolio Optimization has you collect historical stock prices for 20 companies from Yahoo! Finance and calculate the sample means, standard deviations, and correlations. These inputs are feed into the matrix functions of Excel to calculate the efficient frontier, the tangent line, and the weights of the tangent portfolio, and then graph everything. The spreadsheet model in Life-Cycle Financial Planning includes a detailed treatment of federal and state tax schedules, social Security taxes and benefits, etc., which permit the realistic exploration savings, retirement, and investments choices over a lifetime. The spreadsheet model in US Yield Curve Dynamics shows you 30 years of monthly US yield curve history in just a few minutes. Real call and put prices are feed into the Black Scholes Option Pricing model and Excel's Solver to used to back-solve for the implied volatilities. Then the "smile" pattern (or more like a "scowl" pattern) of implied volatilities is graphed. As a practical matter, all of these sophisticated applications require spreadsheet modeling.

- **Annual Updates.** I will be updating this book each year. For the next update, I plan to:
  | Correct any typos that are uncovered (please report typos to **cholden@indiana.edu**).
  | Triple the number of end-of-chapter problems and include a richer variety of problems.
  | Develop an instructors manual with complete solutions for adopting instructors.
  | Update the term structure database by a year.
  | Add a few more spreadsheet models.

Conventions Used In This Book

This book uses a number of conventions.

- **Time Goes Across The Columns And Variables Go Down The Rows.** When something happens over time, I let each column represent a period of time. For example in life-cycle financial planning, date 0 is in column B, date 1 is in column C, date 2 is in column D, etc. Each row represents a different variable, which is usually a labeled in column A. This manner of organizing spreadsheets is so common because it is how financial statements are organized.

- **Color Coding.** A standard color scheme is used to clarify the structure of the spreadsheet models. The printed book uses: (1) light gray shading for input values, (2) no shading (i.e. white) for throughput formulas, and (3) dark gray shading for final results ("the bottom line"). The accompanying electronic version of the book uses: (1) yellow shading for input values, (2) no shading (i.e. white) for throughput formulas, and (3) green shading for final results ("the bottom line"). A few spreadsheets include choice variables. Choice variables use medium gray shading in the printed book and blue shading in the electronic version.

- **The Time Line Technique.** The most natural technique for discounting cash flows in a spreadsheet model is the time line technique, where each column corresponds to a period of time. As an example, see the section labeled **Calculate Bond Price using the Cash Flows** in the figure below.

	A	B	C	D	E	F	G	H	I	J
1	**BOND PRICING**	**Basics**	**Annual Percentage Rate**							
2										
3	**Inputs**									
4	Rate Convention: 1 = EAR, 0 = APR	0								
5	Annual Coupon Rate (CR)	5.0%								
6	Yield to Maturity (Annualized) (y)	9.0%								
7	Number of Payments / Year (NOP)	2								
8	Number of Periods to Maturity (T)	8								
9	Face Value (FV)	$1,000								
10										
11	**Outputs**									
12	Discount Rate / Period (RATE)	4.5%								
13	Coupon Payment (PMT)	$25								
14										
15	**Calculate Bond Price using the Cash Flows**									
16	Period	0	1	2	3	4	5	6	7	8
17	Time (Years)	0.0	0.5	1.0	1.5	2.0	2.5	3.0	3.5	4.0
18	Cash Flows		$25.00	$25.00	$25.00	$25.00	$25.00	$25.00	$25.00	$1,025.00
19	Present Value of Cash Flow		$23.92	$22.89	$21.91	$20.96	$20.06	$19.20	$18.37	$720.76
20	Bond Price	$868.08								
21										
22	**Calculate Bond Price using the Formula**									
23	Bond Price	$868.08								
24										
25	**Calculate Bond Price using the PV Function**									
26	Bond Price	$868.08								
27										
28	**Calculate Bond Price using the PRICE Function (under APR)**									
29	Bond Price	$868.08								

- **Using As Many Different Techniques As Possible.** In the figure above, the bond price is calculated using as many different techniques as possible. Specifically, it is calculated four ways: (1) discounting each cash flow on a time line, (2) using the closed-form formula, (3) using Excel's PV function, and (4) using Excel's more advanced PRICE function (found in Excel's Analysis ToolPak Add-In). This approach makes the point that all four techniques are equivalent. This approach also develops skill at double-checking these calculations, which is a very important method for avoiding errors in practice.

- **Dynamic Charts.** Dynamic charts allow you to see such things as a "movie" of the Term Structure of Interest Rates moves over time or an "animated graph" of how increasing the volatility of an underlying stock increases the value of an option. Dynamic charts are a combination of an up/down arrow (a "spinner") to rapidly change an input and a chart to rapidly display the changing output. I invented dynamic charts back in 1995 and I have included many examples of this useful educational tool throughout this book.

Craig's Challenge

I challenge the readers of this book to dramatically improve your finance education by personally constructing all 43 spreadsheet models in all 20 chapters of this book. This will take you about 22 to 43 hours depending on your current spreadsheet skills. Let me assure you that it will be an excellent investment. You will:

  gain a practical understanding of the core concepts of Fundamentals of Investments,
  develop hands-on, spreadsheet modeling skills, and
  build an entire suite of finance applications, which you fully understand.

When you complete this challenge, I invite you to send an e-mail to me at **cholden@indiana.edu** to share the good news. Please tell me your name, school, (prospective) graduation year, and which spreadsheet modeling book you completed. I will add you to a web-based honor roll at:

http://www.spreadsheetmodeling.com/honor-roll.htm

We can celebrate together!

The Spreadsheet Modeling Series

This book is part a series of book/CDs on **Spreadsheet Modeling** by Craig W. Holden, published by Prentice Hall. The series includes:

| **Spreadsheet Modeling in Corporate Finance**,
| **Spreadsheet Modeling in the Fundamentals of Corporate Finance**,
| **Spreadsheet Modeling in Investments**,
| **Spreadsheet Modeling in the Fundamentals of Investments**, and
| **Spreadsheet Modeling in the Finance** (a mixture of investments and corporate finance).

Each book teaches value-added skills in constructing financial models in Excel. Complete information about the **Spreadsheet Modeling** series is available at my web site:

http://www.spreadsheetmodeling.com

Suggestions for Faculty Members

There are many ways to integrate **Spreadsheet Modeling in the Fundamentals of Investments** into your class:

- Assign the construction of spreadsheet models from the list of problems as graded or ungraded homework.

- Expand or customize the list of problems into major class projects.

- Demonstrate the construction of spreadsheet models in your class.

    o Optionally, have the students follow along on their own laptop computers if you have a policy requiring every student to own a laptop computer or

    o Schedule some class sessions in a computer lab and have students follow along on the lab computers.

- Schedule class sessions a computer lab and have students construct spreadsheet models on their own, but with you and/or your assistant available to answer spreadsheet or finance questions.

- Assign the construction of spreadsheet models as out-of-class projects, but schedule several special "help lab" sessions in a computer lab when you and/or your assistant will be available to answer spreadsheet or finance questions.

    o Optionally, blank-out some cells of the fully-constructed spreadsheets supplied to faculty members, supply this partially-constructed spreadsheet to students, and have them follow the remaining steps to finish it or

    o Optionally, have students write a report to a hypothetical boss, which intuitively explains their method of analysis, key assumptions, and key results.

Alternative Notation Versions

One nice thing about spreadsheets is that you can use long descriptive labels to describe most variables and their corresponding formulas. However, some finance formulas are complex enough that they really require mathematical notation. When this happens, I provide alternative notation versions that match the notation of all popular fundamentals of investments finance textbooks. The spreadsheet below shows the symbols that are used in all notation versions. I have selected the notation to fill in any gaps.

	A	B	C	D	E	F	G	H
1	**SYMBOL LIST**	**All Investment Versions**						
2		Bodie	Corrado	Francis	Haugen	Jones	Reilly	Sharpe
3	**Bonds**							
4	Annual Coupon Rate	CR	CR	CR	CR	CR	CR	CR
5	Yield To Maturity (Annualized)	y	YTM	YTM	Y	YTM	i	y
6	Number of Payments / Period	NOP	NOP	NOP	NOP	NOP	NOP	NOP
7	Number of Periods to Maturity	T	T	T	n	T	T	T
8	Face Value	PAR	FV	PAR	P	MV	P_p	FV
9	Discount Rate / Period	r.	DR	DR	DR	DR	DR	RATE
10	Coupon Payment	PMT	C	PMT	C	PMT	PMT	PMT
11	Bond Price	P	PV	PV	V	P	P_m	P_0
12	Forward Rate from T-1 to T	$f_{T-1,T}$	$f_{T-1,1}$	$FR_{T-1,T}$	$f_{T-1,1}$	$_{t-1}r_1$	$_{t-1}r_1$	$f_{T-1,T}$
13	Duration	D	D	MAC	D_1	D	D	D
14	Modified Duration	D*	D*	MOD	D*	D*	D*	D*
15								
16	**Black-Scholes Option Pricing**							
17	Stock Price	S_0	S	S	V_s	CMP	P_s	P_s
18	Exercise Price	X	K	XP	X	EP	X	E
19	Riskfree Rate	r	r	r	r_F	r.	r.	R
20	Volatility	σ	σ	σ	$\sigma(r)$	σ	σ	σ
21	Time To Maturity	T	T	T	t	t	t	T
22	d_1	d_1	d_1	d_1	d_1	d_1	d_1	d_1
23	d_2	d_2	d_2	d_2	d_2	d_2	d_2	d_2
24	$N(d_1)$	$N(d_1)$	$N(d_1)$	$N(d_1)$	$N(d_1)$	$N(d_1)$	$N(d_1)$	$N(d_1)$
25	$N(d_2)$	$N(d_2)$	$N(d_2)$	$N(d_2)$	$N(d_2)$	$N(d_2)$	$N(d_2)$	$N(d_2)$
26	Call Price	C_0	C	COP	V_c	CP	P_0	V_c
27	Put Price	P_0	P	POP	V_p	PP	P_p	P_p
28	Dividend Yield	d	y	d	d	d	d	d

Acknowledgements

I thank Maureen Riopelle, P.J. Boardman, and Paul Donnelly of Prentice Hall for their vision, innovativeness, and encouragement of **Spreadsheet Modeling in the Fundamentals of Investments**. I thank Alan Bailey, Lori Braumberger, Ryan Brewer, Holly Brown, Cheryl Clayton, Jim Finnegan, Jack Francis, Robert Kleiman, Wendy Liu, Josh McClary, Bill Minic, Melanie Olsen, Wannie Park, Tim Smaby, Gladys Soto, Lauren Tarino, Sorin Tuluca, Marilyn Wiley, and many students for providing helpful comments. I thank my family, Kathryn, Diana, and Jimmy, for their love and support.

READING BOND LISTINGS
BASICS

Problem. Given bond prices and yields as published by the financial press or other information sources, obtain the U.S. Treasury Yield Curve.

Solution Strategy. Collect information about Treasury Bills and Treasury Strips for a variety of different maturity dates. Graph the ask yield of these bonds against their time to maturity. See the figure below.

FIGURE 1.Spreadsheet Model of Reading Bond Listings - Basics.

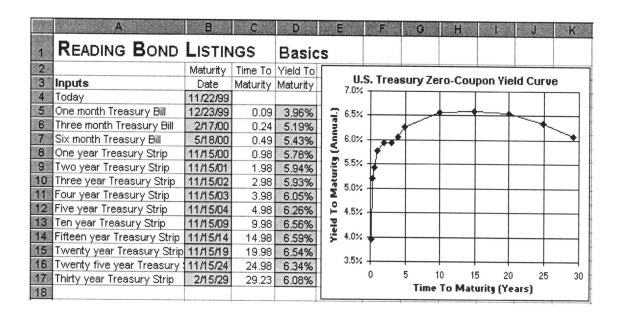

How To Build This Spreadsheet Model.

1.Inputs. Enter the today's date in cell **B4**.We wish to graph the zero-coupon yield curve, so we will use *zero coupon* bonds (i.e., bonds that make a single payment on the maturity date and nothing before then). We will use U.S. Treasury Bills for maturities of less than one year and U.S. Treasury Strips for maturities of one year or more. In the financial press, identify 1, 3, and 6 month Treasury Bills and the 1, 2, 3, 4, 5, 10, 15, 20, 25, and 30 year Treasury Strips. We use more frequent maturities at the short end (1, 3, and 6 month), because often there is more curvature in the yield curve for short maturities. For each Treasury Bill or Treasury Strip, enter the maturity date in the range **B5:B17** and yield to maturity (the "ask yield" column in the *Wall Street Journal*) in the range **D5:D17**. When entering the maturity date, be sure to use four-digit years ("2030"), rather than two-digit years ("30"). Excel assumes that two-digit years in the range 00 to

29 are really 2000 to 2029, but that years in the range 30 to 99 are really 1930 to 1999! This distinction doesn't matter for most applications, but it does matter for long-term bonds maturing in 2030 and beyond!

2.Time To Maturity. For a given bond, Time To Maturity = Maturity Date - Today's Date. We can calculate the fraction of a year between two calendar dates using Excel's Analysis ToolPak Add-In **YEARFRAC** function. Excel's Analysis ToolPak Add-In contains several advanced date functions that are useful in finance.

- Click on **Tools**, **Add-Ins**, check the **Analysis ToolPak** checkbox on the Add-Ins dialog box (see Figure 2 below), and click on **OK**.

FIGURE 2.The Add-Ins dialog box.

- The date function we will use is **YEARFRAC(Today's Date, Maturity Date)**. Enter **=YEARFRAC($B$4,B5)** in cell **C5**. The two $ in **$B$4** lock in the row and column when the cell formula is copied. Copy cell **C5** to the range **C6:C17**.

3.Graph the Yield Curve. Highlight the range**C5:D17**and then choose **Insert Chart** from the main menu. Select an**XY(Scatter)**chart type and make other selections to complete the Chart Wizard.

The November 22nd, 1999 U.S. Treasury Yield Curve demonstrates some frequently-observed properties of the yield curve. Often, there is a sharp rise at the short-end (up to 1 year to maturity), a gentle rise after that, and a small dip at the long-end (past 20 years to maturity).

BOND PRICING
BASICS

Problem. A bond has a face value of $1,000, an annual coupon rate of 5.0%, a yield to maturity of 9.0%, makes 2 (semi-annual) coupon payments per year, and 8 periods to maturity (or 4 years to maturity). What is price of this bond based on the Annual Percentage Rate (APR) convention? What is price of this bond based on the Effective Annual Rate (EAR) convention?

Solution Strategy. We will create a switch that can be used to select either the EAR or APR rate convention. The choice of rate convention will determine the discount rate / period. For a given discount rate / period, we will calculate the bond price in four equivalent ways. First, we will calculate the bond price as the present value of the bond's cash flows. Second, we use a formula for the bond price. Third, we use Excel's **PV** function for a bond price. Fourth, we use Excel's Analysis ToolPak Add-In **PRICE** function, which only works under the APR convention.

FIGURE 1. Spreadsheet Model of Bond Pricing - Basics.

	A	B	C	D	E	F	G	H	I	J
1	**BOND PRICING**	**Basics**		**Annual Percentage Rate**						
2										
3	**Inputs**									
4	Rate Convention: 1 = EAR, 0 = APR	0								
5	Annual Coupon Rate (CR)	5.0%								
6	Yield to Maturity (Annualized) (y)	9.0%								
7	Number of Payments / Year (NOP)	2								
8	Number of Periods to Maturity (T)	8								
9	Face Value (FV)	$1,000								
10										
11	**Outputs**									
12	Discount Rate / Period (RATE)	4.5%								
13	Coupon Payment (PMT)	$25								
14										
15	**Calculate Bond Price using the Cash Flows**									
16	Period	0	1	2	3	4	5	6	7	8
17	Time (Years)	0.0	0.5	1.0	1.5	2.0	2.5	3.0	3.5	4.0
18	Cash Flows		$25.00	$25.00	$25.00	$25.00	$25.00	$25.00	$25.00	$1,025.00
19	Present Value of Cash Flow		$23.92	$22.89	$21.91	$20.96	$20.06	$19.20	$18.37	$720.76
20	Bond Price	$868.08								
21										
22	**Calculate Bond Price using the Formula**									
23	Bond Price	$868.08								
24										
25	**Calculate Bond Price using the PV Function**									
26	Bond Price	$868.08								
27										
28	**Calculate Bond Price using the PRICE Function (under APR)**									
29	Bond Price	$868.08								

How To Build This Spreadsheet Model.

1.Enter The Inputs and Name Them. Enter **0** in cell **B4**. This will serve as a switch between the APR and the EAR rate conventions. To highlight which rate convention is in use, enter **=IF ($B$4=1,"Effective Annual Rate","Annual Percentage Rate")** in cell **D1**. Enter the other inputs into the range **B5:B9** and then name each one. Put the cursor on cell **B5**, click on **Insert, Name, Define,** enter **CR** in the **Names in Workbook** box, and click on **OK**. Put the cursor on cell **B6** and repeat the process to name it **y**. Repeat the process to give the cells **B7**,**B8**, and **B9** the names **NOP, T,** and **FV**, respectively.

2.Calculate the Discount Rate / Period. The Discount Rate / Period depends on the rate convention being used as follows:

$$\text{Discount Rate / Period} = \begin{cases} (1+\text{Yield To Maturity})^{\wedge}\left(1/\left(\text{Number of Payments / Year}\right)\right)-1 & \text{under EAR} \\ \left(\text{Yield To Maturity}\right)/\left(\text{Number of Payments / Year}\right) & \text{under APR} \end{cases}$$

- Enter **=IF($B$4=1,((1+y)^(1/NOP))-1,y/NOP)** in cell **B12** and use the process above to give the cell **B12** the name **RATE**.

3.Calculate the Coupon Payment. The formula is Coupon Payment = Coupon Rate * Face Value / (Number of Payments / Year). Enter **=CR*FV/NOP** in cell **B13** and use the process above to give the cell **B13** the name **PMT** .

4.Calculate Bond Price using the Cash Flows. Calculate the bond price as the present value of the bond's cash flows. This bond has two cash flows per year for four years or eight periods. Enter the period numbers **0,1,2,...,8** in the range**B16:J16**. Complete the bond price calculation as follows:

- Time (years) = (Period) / (Number of Payments / Year) = Period / NOP. Enter **=B16/NOP** in cell **B17** and copy this cell to the range **C17:J17**.

- Cash Flows in Periods 1-7 = Coupon Payment. Enter **=PMT** in cell **C18** and copy this cell to the range **D18:J18**.

- Cash Flow in Period 8 = Coupon Payment + Face Value. Add **+FV** to the formula in cell **J18**, so that it reads **=PMT+FV** .

- Present Value of Cash Flow =(Cash Flow)/((1+Discount Rate/Period)^ Period) = Cash Flow / ((1+ RATE)^Period). Enter **=C18/((1+RATE)^C16)** in cell **C19** and copy this cell to the range **D19:J19**.

- Present Value of the Bond = Sum of all the Present Value of Cash Flows (row 19). Enter **=SUM(C19:J19)** in cell **B20**.

5.Calculate Bond Price using the Formula. The present value of the bond's cash flows can be simplified down to an equivalent formula. The bond price formula is

$$P_0 = \frac{PMT \cdot \left(1 - \left[(1 + RATE)^{-T}\right]\right)}{RATE} + \frac{FV}{(1 + RATE)^{T}}$$

where the first term is the present value of an annuity for the string of coupon payments and the second term is the present value of face value payment at the end. Enter **=PMT*(1-((1+RATE)^(-T)))/RATE+FV/((1+RATE)^T)** in cell **B23**.

6.Calculate Bond Price using the PV Function. Excel has a function to calculate the price of a bond. The format is =-PV(Discount Rate / Period, Number of Periods to Maturity, Coupon Payment, Face Value). Enter **=-PV(RATE,T,PMT,FV)** in cell **B26**.

7.Calculate Bond Price using the PRICE Function (under APR). Excel's Analysis ToolPak Add-In contains several advanced bond functions, including a Bond Price function assuming the APR convention is being used.

- Click on **Tools**, **Add-Ins**, check the **Analysis ToolPak** checkbox on the **Add-Ins** dialog box (see Figure 2 below), and click on **OK**.

FIGURE 2. The Add-Ins dialog box.

- The bond price function is =PRICE(Settlement Date, Maturity Date, Annual Coupon Rate, Yield To Maturity, Redemption Value, Number of Payments). The Settlement Date is the date when you exchange money to purchase the bond. Specifying the exact day of settlement and maturity allows a very precise calculation. For our purpose, we simple want the difference between the two dates to equal the (8 Periods To Maturity) / (2 Payments / Year) = 4 Years To Maturity. This is easily accomplished by the use of the DATE function. The DATE Function has the format =DATE(Year, Month, Day). We will enter an arbitrary starting date of 1/1/2000 for the Settlement Date and then specify a formula for 1/1/2000 plus T / NOP for the Maturity Date. We need to add an IF statement to test for the rate convention being used. The bond function is only valid with APR. Enter **=IF($B$4=1,"", PRICE(DATE(2000,1,1), DATE (2000+T/NOP,1,1), CR,y,100,NOP) * FV/100)** in cell **B29**. This uses a conventional Redemption Value of $100.00 and scales the resulting price by the ratio of (FV Value) / $100.00.

The resulting bond price is $868.08. Notice you get the same answer all four ways: using the cash flows, using the formula, using the PV function, or using the PRICE function!

BOND PRICING
By Yield To Maturity

What is the relationship between bond price and yield to maturity? We can construct a graph to find out.

FIGURE 1. Spreadsheet Model of Bond Pricing - By Yield To Maturity.

How To Build This Spreadsheet Model.

1.Start with the Basics Spreadsheet and Delete Rows. Open the spreadsheet that you created for Bond Pricing - Basics and immediately save the spreadsheet under a new name using the **File Save As** command. Delete rows **15** through **29** by selecting the range **A15:A29**, clicking on **Edit**, **Delete**, selecting the **Entire Row** radio button on the **Delete** dialog box, and clicking on **OK**.

2.Enter Yield To Maturity (Annualized). Enter Yield To Maturity values **1.0%**, **2.0%**, **3.0%**, **4.0%**, ..., **20%** in the range **B16:U16**.

3.Calculate Discount Rate / Period. Copy the Discount Rate / Period formula from cell **B12** to the cell **B17**. In cell **B17**, change the variable **y** to **B16**, so that the formula reads =IF($B$4=1, ((1+B16)^(1/NOP))-1,B16/NOP) and copy the cell **B17** to the range **C17:U17**.

4.Calculate Bond Price. Calculate the bond price using PV function and the inputs **T**, **PMT**, **FV**, and the Discount Rate / Period in cell **B17**. Enter **=-PV(B17,T,PMT,FV)** in cell **B18** and copy the cell to the range **C18:U18**.

5.Graph the Bond Price By Yield To Maturity. Highlight the range **B16:U16** and then while holding down the **Ctrl** button highlight the ranges **B18:U18**. Next choose **Insert Chart** from the main menu. Select an **XY(Scatter)** chart type and make other selections to complete the Chart Wizard. Place the graph in the range **C2:J15**.

This graph shows the inverse relationship between bond price and yield to maturity. In other word, a higher discount rate (yield to maturity) lowers the present value of the bond's cash flows (price). The graph also that the relationship is curved (nonlinear) rather than being a straight line (linear).

BOND PRICING
System of Five Bond Variables

There is a system of five bond variables: (1) Number of Periods to Maturity (T),(2) Face Value (FV), (3) Discount Rate / Period (RATE), (4) Coupon Payments (PMT), and (5) Bond Price (P0) Given any four of these variables, the fifth variable can be found by using Excel functions (and in some cases by formulas).

FIGURE 1. Spreadsheet Model of Bond Pricing - System of Five Bond Variables

	A	B	C	D	E	F	G	H	I
1	**BOND PRICING**	**System of Five Bond Variables**			**Annual Percentage Rate**				
2									
3	Inputs								
4	Rate Convention: 1 = EAR, 0 = APR	0							
5	Annual Coupon Rate (CR)	5.0%							
6	Yield to Maturity (Annualized) (y)	9.0%							
7	Number of Payments / Year (NOP)	2							
8	**(1) Number of Periods to Maturity (T)**	8							
9	**(2) Face Value (FV)**	$1,000							
10	**(3) Discount Rate / Period (RATE)**	4.5%							
11	**(4) Coupon Payment (PMT)**	$25							
12	**(5) Bond Price (P0)**	$868.08							
13									
14	**(1) Number of Periods to Maturity (T)**								
15	Number of Periods to Maturity using the NPER Function	8							
16									
17	**(2) Face Value (FV)**								
18	Face Value using the FV Function	$1,000.00							
19	Face Value using the Formula	$1,000.00							
20									
21	**(3) Find Discount Rate / Period (RATE)**								
22	Discount Rate / Period using the RATE Function	4.5%							
23									
24	**(4) Coupon Payment (PMT)**								
25	Coupon Payment using the PMT Function	$25.00							
26	Coupon Payment using the Formula	$25.00							
27									
28	**(5) Bond Price (P0)**								
29	Bond Price using the P0 Function	$868.08							
30	Bond Price using the Formula	$868.08							

How To Build This Spreadsheet Model.

1.Start with the Basics Spreadsheet and Delete Rows. Open the spreadsheet that you created for Bond Pricing - Basics and immediately save the spreadsheet under a new name using the **File Save As** command. Delete rows **27** through **29** by selecting the range **A27:A29**, clicking on **Edit**, **Delete**, selecting the **Entire Row** radio button on the **Delete** dialog box, and clicking on **OK**. Then repeat this procedure to delete rows **14** through **25** and repeat this procedure again to delete rows **10** through **11**. This places the five bond variables in rows **8** through **12**, highlighted with **purple labels** above.

2.Calculate Number of Periods to Maturity (T). NPER is the Excel function to calculate the number of periods to maturity. The format is =NPER(Discount Rate / Period, Coupon Payment, -Bond Price, FV Value). Enter **=NPER(RATE,PMT,-P0,FV)** in cell **B15**.

3.Calculate Face Value (FV). There are two ways to calculate the face value of the bond.

- Use the Excel Function FV. The format is =FV(Discount Rate / Period, Number of Periods to Maturity, Coupon Payment, -Bond Price). Enter **=FV(RATE,T,PMT,-P0)** in cell **B18**.

- Use the face value formula:

$$FV = P_0 \cdot \left(1 + RATE\right)^T - \frac{PMT \cdot \left(\left[\left(1 + RATE\right)^T\right] - 1\right)}{RATE}$$

  where the first term is the future value of the bond price and the second term is the future values of the string of coupon payments. Enter **=P0*((1+RATE)^T)-PMT*(((1+RATE)^T)-1)/RATE** in cell **B19**.

4.Calculate Discount Rate / Period (RATE). RATE is the Excel function to calculate the discount rate per period. The format is =RATE(Number of Periods to Maturity, Coupon Payment, -Bond Price, FV Value). Enter **=RATE(T,PMT,-P0,FV)** in cell **B22**.

5.Calculate Coupon Payment (PMT). There are two ways to calculate the coupon payment of the bond.

- Use the Excel Function PMT. The format is =PMT(Discount Rate / Period, Number of Periods to Maturity, -Bond Price, FV Value). Enter **=PMT(RATE,T,-P0,FV)** in cell **B25**.

- Use the coupon payment formula:

$$PMT = \frac{P_0 - FV / \left(1 + RATE\right)^T}{\left(1 - \left(\left(1 + RATE\right)^{-T}\right)\right) / RATE}$$

  where the numerator is the bond price minus the present value of the FV value and the denominator is the present value of a \$1 coupon payment. Enter **=(P0-FV/((1+RATE)^T)) /((1-((1+RATE)^(-T))) /RATE)** in cell **B26**.

6.Calculate Bond Price (P0). There are two ways to calculate the price of the bond.

- Use the Excel Function PV. The format is =PV(Discount Rate / Period, Number of Periods to Maturity, Coupon Payment, FV Value). Enter **=-PV(RATE,T,PMT,FV)** in cell **B29**.

- Use the coupon payment formula:

$$P_0 = \frac{PMT \cdot \left(1 - \left[\left(1 + RATE\right)^{-T}\right]\right)}{RATE} + \frac{FV}{\left(1 + RATE\right)^T}$$

where the first term is the present value of the string of coupon payments and the second term is the present value of the FV value. Enter **=PMT*(1-((1+RATE)^ (T)))/RATE+FV/((1+RATE)^T)** in cell **B30**.

We see that the system of five bond variables is internally consistent. The five outputs in rows 15 through 30 (T=8, FV=1000, RATE=4.5%, PMT=$25, P0=$868.08) are identical to the five inputs in rows **8** through **12** . Thus, any of the five bond variables can be calculated from the other four in a fully consistent manner.

BOND PRICING
Dynamic Chart

If you increased the coupon rate of a bond, what would happen to its price? If you increased the yield to maturity of a bond, what would happen to its price? You can answer these questions and more by creating a *Dynamic Chart* using "spinners." Spinners are up-arrow / down-arrow buttons that allow you to easily change the inputs to the model with the click of a mouse. Then the spreadsheet recalculates the model and instantly redraws the model outputs on the graph.

FIGURE 1. Spreadsheet Model of Bond Pricing - Dynamic Chart.

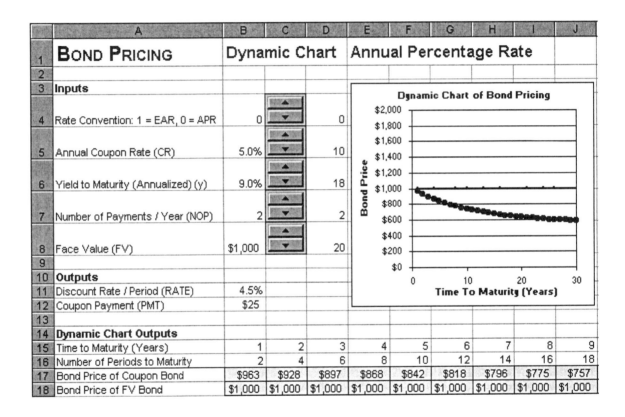

	A	B	C	D	E	F	G	H	I	J
1	**BOND PRICING**	Dynamic Chart			Annual Percentage Rate					
2										
3	Inputs									
4	Rate Convention: 1 = EAR, 0 = APR	0		0						
5	Annual Coupon Rate (CR)	5.0%		10						
6	Yield to Maturity (Annualized) (y)	9.0%		18						
7	Number of Payments / Year (NOP)	2		2						
8	Face Value (FV)	$1,000		20						
9										
10	Outputs									
11	Discount Rate / Period (RATE)	4.5%								
12	Coupon Payment (PMT)	$25								
13										
14	Dynamic Chart Outputs									
15	Time to Maturity (Years)	1	2	3	4	5	6	7	8	9
16	Number of Periods to Maturity	2	4	6	8	10	12	14	16	18
17	Bond Price of Coupon Bond	$963	$928	$897	$868	$842	$818	$796	$775	$757
18	Bond Price of FV Bond	$1,000	$1,000	$1,000	$1,000	$1,000	$1,000	$1,000	$1,000	$1,000

How To Build This Spreadsheet Model.

1. **Start with the Basics Spreadsheet and Delete Rows.** Open the spreadsheet that you created for Bond Pricing - Basics and immediately save the spreadsheet under a new name using the **File Save As** command. Delete rows **15** through **29** by selecting the range **A15:A29**, clicking on **Edit**, **Delete**, selecting the **Entire Row** radio button on the **Delete** dialog box, and clicking on **OK** Repeat this procedure to delete row **8**.

2.Increase Row Height for the Spinners. Select the range **A4:A8**. Then click on **Format Row Height** from the main menu. Enter a height of **30** and click on **OK**.

3.Display the Forms Toolbar. Click on **View, Toolbars, Forms** from the main menu.

4.Create the Spinners. Look for the up-arrow / down-arrow button on the **Forms** toolbar (which will display the word **"Spinner"** if you hover the cursor over it) and click on it. Then draw the box for a spinner from the upper left corner of cell **C4** down to the lower right corner of the cell. Then a spinner appears in the cell **C4**. Right click on the spinner (press the right mouse button while the cursor is above the spinner) and a small menu pops up. Click on **Copy**. Then select the cell **C5** and click on **Paste**. This creates an identical spinner in the cell **C5**. Repeat the process three times more. Select cell **C6** and click on **Paste**. Then select cell **C7** and click on **Paste**. Then select cell **C8** and click on **Paste**. You now have five spinners down column **C**.

5.Create The Cell Links. Right click on the first spinner in the cell **C4** and a small menu pops up. Click on **Format Control** and a dialog box pops up. Click on the **Control** tab, then enter the cell link **D4** in the **Cell link** edit box and click on **OK**. Repeat this procedure for the other four spinners. Link the spinner in cell **C5** to cell **D5**. Link the spinner in cell **C6** to cell **D6**. Link the spinner in cell **C7** to cell **D7**. Link the spinner in cell **C8** to cell **D8** and also on the **Control tab**, set the **Minimum value** equal to **1** . Test your spinners by clicking on the up-arrows and down-arrows of the spinners to see how they change the values in the linked cells.

6.Create Scaled Inputs. The values in the linked cells are always integers, but they can be scaled appropriately to the problem at hand. Restrict the value in cell **B4** to be either 1 or 0 by entering **=IF(D4>1,1,D4)**. In cell **B5**, enter **=D5/200**. In cell **B6**, enter **=D6/200**. In cell **B7**, enter **=D7**. In cell **B8**, enter **=D8*50**.

7.Enter Time To Maturity. Enter Time To Maturity values **1, 2, 3, 4, ..., 30** in the range **B15:AE15**.

8.Calculate Number of Periods to Maturity. The Number of Periods to Maturity = (Time to Maturity) * (Number of Periods / Year). In cell **B16**, enter **=B15*NOP** and copy the cell **B16** to the range **C16:AE16**.

9.Calculate Bond Price of a Coupon Bond. Calculate the duration of a coupon bond using the **PV** bond duration function and the scaled inputs in cells **RATE, PMT, PAR** and the Time to Maturity in cell **B16**. Specifically, enter **=-PV(RATE,B$16,PMT,FV)** in cell **B17**. Be sure that **B$16** has a $ in the middle to lock in the row, but not the column.

10.Calculate Bond Price of a Par Bond. A par bond is a bond with a coupon rate equal to the yield to maturity. As a benchmark for comparison, calculate the bond price of a par bond using the same inputs for everything else. Copy the formula in cell **B17** to cell **B18**. Then change the coupon payment from **PMT** to **RATE*FV** so that the formula reads **=-PV (RATE,B$16,RATE*FV,FV)**. Copy the range **B17:B18** to the range **C17:AE18**.

11.Graph the Bond Price of a Coupon Bond and Par Bond. Highlight the range **B15:AE15** and then while holding down the **Ctrl** button highlight the range **B17:AE18**. Next choose **Insert Chart** from the main menu. Select an **XY(Scatter)** chart type and make other selections to complete the Chart Wizard. Place the graph in the range **E3:J12**.

Your *Dynamic Chart* allows you to change the Bond Price inputs and instantly see the impact on a graph of the price of a coupon bond and par bond by time to maturity. This allows you to perform instant experiments on Bond Price. Below is a list of experiments that you might want to perform:

- What happens when the annual coupon rate is increased?

- What happens when the yield to maturity is increased?

- What happens when the number of payments / year is increased?

- What happens when the face value is increased?

- What is the relationship between the price of a par bond and time to maturity?

- What happens when the annual coupon rate is increased to the point that it equals the yield to maturity?

- What happens when it is increased further?

BOND PRICING
Problems

Problems To Build And Use The Spreadsheet Models

1. A bond has a face value of $1,000, an annual coupon rate of 4.60%, an yield to maturity of 8.1%, makes 2 (semi-annual) coupon payments per year, and 10 periods to maturity (or 5 years to maturity). Build the **Bond Pricing - Basics** model and use it to determine the price of this bond based on the Annual Percentage Rate (APR) convention and the price of this bond based on the Effective Annual Rate (EAR) convention.

2. Build the **Bond Pricing - By Yield To Maturity** model and use it to determine the relationship between bond price and yield to maturity by constructing a graph of the relationship.

3. Build the **Bond Pricing - System Of Five Bond Variables** model and use it with four of the bond variables to determine the fifth bond variable.

   a. Given Number of Periods to Maturity is 10, Face Value is $1,000, Discount Rate / Period is 3.2%, and Coupon Payment is $40, determine the Bond Price.
   b. Given Number of Periods to Maturity is 8, Face Value is $1,000, Discount Rate / Period is 4.5%, and the Bond Price is $880.00, determine the Coupon Payment.
   c. Given Number of Periods to Maturity is 6, Face Value is $1,000, Coupon Payment is $30, and the Bond Price is $865.00, determine Discount Rate / Period.
   d. Given Number of Periods to Maturity is 8, Discount Rate / Period is 3.8%, Coupon Payment is $45, and the Bond Price is $872.00, determine Face Value.
   e. Given Face Value is $1,000, Discount Rate / Period is 4.3%, Coupon Payment is $37, and the Bond Price is $887.00, determine the Number of Periods to Maturity. Ê

4. Build the **Bond Pricing - Dynamic Chart** model and use it to perform instant experiments on whether changing various inputs causes an increase or decrease in the Bond Price and by how much.

   a. What happens when the annual coupon rate is increased?
   b. What happens when the yield to maturity is increased?
   c. What happens when the number of payments / year is increased?
   d. What happens when the face value is increased?
   e. What is the relationship between the price of a par bond and time to maturity?
   f. What happens when the annual coupon rate is increased to the point that it equals the yield to maturity? What happens when it is increased further?

BOND DURATION
Basics

Problem. A bond has a face value of $1,000 , an annual coupon rate of 5.0% , a yield to maturity of 9.0% , makes 2(semi-annual) coupon payments per year, and 8 periods to maturity (or 4 years to maturity). What is duration and modified duration of this bond based on the Annual Percentage Rate (APR) convention? What is duration and modified duration of this bond based on the Effective Annual Rate (EAR) convention? What is the intuitive interpretation of duration?

Solution Strategy. The choice of either the EAR or APR rate convention will determine the discount rate / period. For a given the discount rate / period, we will calculate duration and modified duration three equivalent ways. First, we will calculate duration as the weighted-average time to the bond's cash flows. This method illustrates the intuitive interpretation of duration. Second, we use a formula for duration. In both cases, modified duration is a simple adjustment of regular duration (also called Macaulay's Duration). Third, we use Excel's Analysis ToolPak Add-In **DURATION** and **MDURATION** functions, which only work under the APR convention.

FIGURE 1. Spreadsheet Model of Bond Duration - Basics.

	A	B	C	D	E	F	G	H	I	J	K
1	**BOND DURATION**	**Basics**			**Annual Percentage Rate**						
2											
3	**Inputs**										
4	Rate Convention: 1 = EAR, 0 = APR	0									
5	Annual Coupon Rate (CR)	5.0%									
6	Yield to Maturity (Annualized) (y)	9.0%									
7	Number of Payments / Year (NOP)	2									
8	Number of Periods to Maturity (T)	8									
9	Face Value (FV)	$1,000									
10											
11	**Outputs**										
12	Discount Rate / Period (RATE)	4.5%									
13	Coupon Payment (PMT)	$25									
14											
15	**Calculate Bond Duration using the Cash Flows**										
16	Period	0	1	2	3	4	5	6	7	8	
17	Time (Years)	0.0	0.5	1.0	1.5	2.0	2.5	3.0	3.5	4.0	Total
18	Cash Flows		$25.00	$25.00	$25.00	$25.00	$25.00	$25.00	$25.00	$1,025.00	
19	Present Value of Cash Flow		$23.92	$22.89	$21.91	$20.96	$20.06	$19.20	$18.37	$720.76	$868.08
20	Weight		2.8%	2.6%	2.5%	2.4%	2.3%	2.2%	2.1%	83.0%	100.0%
21	Weight * Time		0.01	0.03	0.04	0.05	0.06	0.07	0.07	3.32	3.65
22	Duration	3.65									
23	Modified Duration	3.49									
24											
25	**Calculate Bond Duration using the Formula**										
26	Duration	3.65									
27	Modified Duration	3.49									
28											
29	**Calculate Bond Duration using the Function (under APR)**										
30	Duration	3.65									
31	Modified Duration	3.49									

How To Build This Spreadsheet Model.

1.Enter The Inputs and Name Them. Enter **0** in cell **B4**. This will serve as a switch between the APR and the EAR rate conventions. To highlight which rate convention is in use, enter **=IF ($B$4=1,"Effective Annual Rate", "Annual Percentage Rate")** in cell **E1**. Enter the other inputs into the range **B5:B9** and then name each one. Put the cursor on cell **B5**, click on **Insert, Name, Define**, enter **CR** in the **Names in Workbook** box, and click on **OK** Put the cursor on cell **B6** and repeat the process to name it **y**. Repeat the process to give the cells **B7, B8** , and **B9** the names **NOP, T**, and **FV**, respectively.

2.Calculate the Discount Rate / Period. The Discount Rate / Period depends on the rate convention being used as follows:

$$\text{Discount Rate / Period} = \begin{cases} (1+\text{Yield To Maturity})^{\wedge}(1/(\text{Number of Payments / Year}))-1 & \text{under EAR} \\ (\text{Yield To Maturity})/(\text{Number of Payments / Year}) & \text{under APR} \end{cases}$$

Enter **=IF($B$4=1,((1+y)^(1/NOP))-1,y/NOP)** in cell **B12** and use the process above to give the cell **B12** the name **RATE**.

3.Calculate the Coupon Payment. The formula is Coupon Payment = Coupon Rate * Face Value / (Number of Payments / Year). Enter **=CR*FV/NOP** in cell **B13** and use the process above to give the cell **B13** the name **PMT**.

4.Calculate Bond Duration using the Cash Flows. Calculating duration as a weighted-average time to cash flows directly illustrates the key intuition for duration. This bond has two cash flows per year for four years or eight periods. Enter the period numbers **0, 1, 2, ..., 8** in the range **B16:J16**. Complete the duration calculation as follows:

- Time (years) = (Period) / (Number of Payments / Year) = Period / NOP. Enter **=B16/NOP** in cell **B17** and copy this cell to the range **C17:J17**.

- Cash Flows in Periods 1-7 = Coupon Payment. Enter **=PMT** in cell **C18** and copy this cell to the range **D18:J18**.

- Cash Flow in Period 8 = Same as above + Face Value. Add **+FV** to the formula in cell **J18**, so that it reads **=PMT+FV**.

- Present Value of Cash Flow =(Cash Flow)/((1+(Discount Rate / Period))^ Period) = Cash Flow / ((1+ RATE)^Period). Enter **=C18/((1+RATE)^C16)** in cell **C19** and copy this cell to the range **D19:J19**.

- Present Value of the Bond = Sum of all the Present Value of Cash Flows (row 19). Enter **=SUM(C19:J19)** in cell **K19**.

- Weight on date t = Present Value of Cash Flow on date t / Present Value of the Bond. Enter **=C19/$K$19** in cell **C20** and copy this cell to the range **D20:K20**.

- Weight * Time. Enter **=C20*C17** in cell **C21** and copy this cell to the range **D21:J21**.

- (Macaulay's) Duration = Sum of all the Weight * Time variables (row 21). Enter **=SUM (C21:J21)** in cell **B22**. Optionally for completeness, enter the same formula in cell **K21**.

- Modified Duration = Duration / (1+(Discount Rate / Period)) = Duration / (1 + RATE). Enter **=B22/(1+RATE)** in cell **B23**.

This method of calculation directly illustrates the key intuition that (Macaulay's) duration is the weighted-average of the time until cash flows are received. The weights are based on the ratio of the present value of each cash flow over the present value of the total bond.

5.Calculate Bond Duration using the Formula. The weighted-average time calculation can be simplified down to an equivalent formula solution for (Macaulay's) duration.

- The duration formula is

$$D = \frac{1+RATE}{RATE \cdot NOP} - \frac{1+RATE+T \cdot (CR / NOP - RATE)}{CR \cdot \left[(1+RATE)^T - 1 \right] + RATE \cdot NOP}$$

Enter **=(1+RATE)/(RATE*NOP)-(1+RATE+T*(CR/NOP-RATE))/(CR*((1+RATE)^T-1)+RATE*NOP)** in cell **B26**.

- Modified Duration uses the same formula as above. Copy the formula in cell **B23** to cell **B27**.

6.Calculate Bond Duration by Function. Excel's Analysis ToolPak Add-In contains several advanced bond functions, including duration and modified duration.

- Click on **Tools**, **Add-Ins**, check the **Analysis ToolPak** checkbox on the **Add-Ins** dialog box (see Figure 2 below), and click on **OK**.

FIGURE 2. The Add-Ins dialog box.

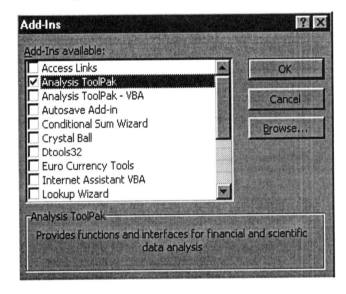

- The duration function is =DURATION(Settlement Date, Maturity Date, Annual Coupon Rate, Yield To Maturity, Number of Payments). The Settlement Date is the date when you exchange money to purchase the bond. Specifying the exact day of settlement and maturity allows a very precise calculation. For our purpose, we simple want the difference between the two dates to equal the (8 Periods To Maturity) / (2 Payments / Year) = 4 Years To Maturity. This is easily accomplished by the use of the DATE function. The DATE Function has the format =DATE(Year, Month, Day). We will enter an arbitrary starting date of 1/1/2000 for the Settlement Date and then specify a formula for 1/1/2000 plus T / NOP for the Maturity Date. We need to add an IF statement to test for the rate convention being used. The duration and modified duration functions are only valid with APR. Enter **=IF($B$4=1,"", DURATION(DATE(2000,1,1), DATE(2000+T/NOP,1,1), CR,y,NOP))** in cell **B30**.

- The modified duration function is =MDURATION(Settlement Date, Maturity Date, Annual Coupon Rate, Yield To Maturity, Number of Payments) and has identical arguments. Enter **=IF($B$4=1,"", MDURATION(DATE(2000,1,1), DATE(2000+T/NOP,1,1), CR,y,NOP))** in cell **B31**.

The duration is 3.65 years and the modified duration is 3.49 years. Notice you get the same answer all three ways: using the cash flows, using the formula, or using the Analysis ToolPak Add-In function!

BOND DURATION
Price Sensitivity using Duration

Bond duration is a measure of the price sensitivity of a bond to changes in interest rates. In other words, it is a measure of the bond's interest rate risk. Duration tells you approximately what percent change in bond price will result from a given change in yield to maturity. The duration approximation can be shown on a graph and compared to the actual percent change in the bond price.

FIGURE 1. Spreadsheet Model of Bond Duration - Price Sensitivity using Duration

	A	B	C	D	E	F	G	H	I	J
1	**BOND DURATION**	**Price Sensitivity Using Duration**								
2		**Annual Percentage Rate**								
3	**Inputs**									
4	Rate Convention: 1 = EAR, 0 = APR	0								
5	Annual Coupon Rate (CR)	5.0%								
6	Yield to Maturity (Annualized) (y)	9.0%								
7	Number of Payments / Year (NOP)	2								
8	Number of Periods to Maturity (T)	8								
9	Face Value (FV)	$1,000								
10										
11	**Outputs**									
12	Discount Rate / Period (RATE)	4.5%								
13	Coupon Payment (PMT)	$25								
14										
15										
16										
17										
18										
19										
20	**Graph Outputs**									
21	Yield to Maturity (Annualized)	1.0%	2.0%	3.0%	4.0%	5.0%	6.0%	7.0%	8.0%	9.0%
22	Discount Rate / Period	0.5%	1.0%	1.5%	2.0%	2.5%	3.0%	3.5%	4.0%	4.5%
23	Change in Yield to Maturity	-8.0%	-7.0%	-6.0%	-5.0%	-4.0%	-3.0%	-2.0%	-1.0%	0.0%
24	Actual Bond Price	$1,156	$1,115	$1,075	$1,037	$1,000	$965	$931	$899	$868
25	Current Bond Price	$868	$868	$868	$868	$868	$868	$868	$868	$868
26	Actual Percent Change in Price	33.2%	28.4%	23.8%	19.4%	15.2%	11.2%	7.3%	3.6%	0.0%
27	Modified Duration	3.49	3.49	3.49	3.49	3.49	3.49	3.49	3.49	3.49
28	Duration Approximation	27.9%	24.4%	20.9%	17.4%	14.0%	10.5%	7.0%	3.5%	0.0%

How To Build This Spreadsheet Model.

1. Start with the Basics Spreadsheet and Delete Rows. Open the spreadsheet that you created for Bond Duration - Basics and immediately save the spreadsheet under a new name using the **File Save As** command. Delete rows **27** through **31** by selecting the range **A27:A31**, clicking on **Edit**, **Delete**, selecting the **Entire Row** radio button on the **Delete** dialog box, and clicking on **OK** Repeat this procedure to delete rows **14** through **25**.

20

2.Yield To Maturity (Annualized). Enter Yield To Maturity values **1.0%, 2.0%, 3.0%, 4.0%, ..., 20.0%** in the range **B21:U21**.

3.Discount Rate / Period. The Discount Rate / Period depends on the rate convention being used as follows:

$$\text{Discount Rate / Period} = \begin{cases} (1+\text{Yield To Maturity})^{\wedge}(1/(\text{Number of Payments / Year}))-1 & \text{under EAR} \\ (\text{Yield To Maturity})/(\text{Number of Payments / Year}) & \text{under APR} \end{cases}$$

Enter **IF($B$4=1,((1+B21)^(1/NOP))-1,B21/NOP)** in cell **B22** and copy the cell **B22** to the range **C22:U22**.

4.Change in Yield To Maturity. The Change in Yield To Maturity = New Yield To Maturity - Current Yield To Maturity (y). In cell **B23**, enter **=B21-y** and copy the cell **B23** to the range **C23:U23**.

5.Actual Bond Price. Calculate the bond price using the inputs **T, PMT, FV,** and the Discount Rate / Period in cell **B22**. Specifically, enter **=-PV(B22,T,PMT,FV)** in cell **B24** and copy the cell **B24** to the range **C24:U24**.

6.Current Bond Price. Calculate the bond price using the original inputs. Copy the formula in cell **B24** to cell **B25**. Then change the yield to maturity from **B23** to **RATE** so that the formula reads **=-PV(RATE,T,PMT,FV)** and copy the cell **B25** to the range **C25:U25**.

7.Actual Percent Change in Price. The percent Actual Percent Change in Price = (Actual Bond Price -Current Bond Price) / Current Bond Price. In cell **B26**, enter **=(B24-B25)/B25** and copy the cell **B26** to the range **C26:U26**.

8.Modified Duration. Calculate modified duration in two steps. First, copy the duration formula in cell **B14** to cell **B27**. Then change the formula to modified duration by adding **(** at the beginning of the formula and adding **)/(1+RATE)** at the end of the formula. Thus, the modified duration formula in cell **B27** will look like **=((1+RATE)/(RATE*NOP)-(1+RATE+T* (CR/NOP-RATE))/(CR* ((1+RATE)^T-1)+RATE*NOP))/(1+RATE)**. Then copy the cell **B27** to the range **C27:U27**. Delete the content of the range **A14:B14** by selecting the range and then pressing the **Delete** key.

9.Duration Approximation. The Duration Approximation of the Percent Change in Price = - Modified Duration * Change in Yield To Maturity. In cell **B28**, enter **=-B27*B23** and copy the cell **B28** to the range **C28:U28**.

10.Graph the Actual Percent Change in Price and the Duration Approximation. Highlight the range **A23:U23** and then while holding down the **Ctrl** button highlight the ranges **A26:U26** and **A28:U28**. Next choose **Insert Chart** from the main menu. Select an **XY(Scatter)** chart type and make other selections to complete the Chart Wizard. Place the graph in the range **C3:J20**.

It is clear from the graph that duration does a very good job of approximating the price sensitivity of a bond. That is, the percent change in bond price from the duration approximation is very close to the actual percent change. This is especially true for relatively small changes in yield to maturity (say, plus or minus 3%). For larger changes in yield to maturity, there is a gap between the duration approximation and the actual percent change. The gap comes from the fact that the actual percent change is curved, whereas the duration approximation is a straight line. One could do a better job of approximating the price sensitivity of a bond for larger changes in yield to maturity if one could account for the curvature. That is exactly what bond convexity does. To see what kind of improvement you can get by using convexity, check out Bond Convexity - Price Sensitivity using Duration and Convexity.

BOND DURATION
Dynamic Chart

If you increased the coupon rate of a bond, what would happen to it's duration? If you increased the yield to maturity of a bond, what would happen to it's duration? You can answer these questions and more by creating an *Dynamic Chart* using "spinners." Spinners are up-arrow / down-arrow buttons that allow you to easily change the inputs to the model with the click of a mouse. Then the spreadsheet recalculates the model and instantly redraws the model outputs on the graph.

FIGURE 1. Spreadsheet Model of Bond Duration - Dynamic Chart.

How To Build This Spreadsheet Model.

1.Start with the Basics Spreadsheet and Delete Rows. Open the spreadsheet that you created for Bond Duration - Basics and immediately save the spreadsheet under a new name using the **File Save As** command. Delete rows **27** through **31** by selecting the range **A27:A31**, clicking on **Edit**, **Delete**, selecting the **Entire Row** radio button on the **Delete** dialog box, and clicking on **OK**. Repeat this procedure to delete rows **13** through **25**.Repeat this procedure to delete rows **9** through **10**.

2.Increase Row Height for the Spinners. Select the range **A4:A7**. Then click on **Format Row Height** from the main menu. Enter a height of **30** and click on **OK**.

3.Display the Forms Toolbar. Click on **View**, **Toolbars**, **Forms** from the main menu.

4.Create the Spinners. Look for the up-arrow / down-arrow button on the **Forms** toolbar (which will display the word "**Spinner**" if you hover the cursor over it) and click on it. Then draw the box for a spinner from the upper left corner of cell **C4** down to the lower right corner of the cell. Then a spinner appears in the cell **C4**. Right click on the spinner (press the right mouse button while the cursor is above the spinner) and a small menu pops up. Click on **Copy**. Then select the cell **C5** and click on **Paste**. This creates an identical spinner in the cell **C5**. Repeat the process twice more. Select cell **C6** and click on **Paste**. Select cell **C7** and click on **Paste**. You now have four spinners down column **C**.

5.Create The Cell Links. Right click on the first spinner in the cell **C4** and a small menu pops up. Click on **Format Control** and a dialog box pops up. Click on the **Control** tab, then enter the cell link **D4** in the **Cell link** edit box and click on **OK**. Repeat this procedure for the other three spinners. Link the spinner in cell **C5** to cell **D5**. Link the spinner in cell **C6** to cell **D6**. Link the spinner in cell **C7** to cell **D7** and also on the **Control tab**, set the **Minimum value** equal to **1**. Test your spinners by clicking on the up-arrows and down-arrows of the spinners to see how they change the values in the linked cells.

6.Create Scaled Inputs. The values in the linked cells are always integers, but they can be scaled appropriately to the problem at hand. Restrict the value in cell **B4** to be either 1 or 0 by entering **=IF(D4>1,1,D4)**. In cell **B5**, enter **=D5/200**. In cell **B6**, enter **=D6/200**. In cell **B7**, enter **=D7**.

7.Time To Maturity. Enter Time To Maturity values **1, 2, 3, 4, ..., 30** in the range **B13:AE13**.

8.Number of Periods to Maturity. The Number of Periods to Maturity = (Time to Maturity) * (Number of Periods / Year). In cell **B14**, enter **=B13*NOP** and copy the cell **B14** to the range **C14:AE14**.

9.Duration of a Coupon Bond. Copy the duration formula from cell **B11** to cell **B15**. Edit cell **B15** to change the Number of Periods To Maturity from **T** to **B$14** so that the formula reads **= (1+RATE)/(RATE*NOP)-(1+RATE+B$14*(CR/NOP-RATE))/(CR*((1+RATE)^B$14-1) +RATE*NOP)**. Be sure that **B$14** has a $ in the middle to lock in the row, but not the column. Then copy the cell **B15** to the range **C15:U15**.

10.Duration of a Zero Coupon Bond. A zero coupon bond is a bond with a coupon rate equal to 0.0%. As a benchmark for comparison, calculate the duration of a zero-coupon bond using the same inputs for everything else. Copy the formula in cell **B15** to cell **B16**. Then change the coupon rate from **CR** to **0** so that the formula reads **=(1+RATE)/(RATE*NOP) - (1+RATE+B$14* (0/NOP-RATE)) / (0*((1+RATE)^B$14-1)+RATE*NOP)**. Copy the cell **B16** to the range **C16:AE16**.

11.Clean Up. Delete the contents of the range **A8:B8** by selecting the range and then pressing the **Delete** key. Similarly, delete the contents of the range **A11:B11** by selecting the range and then pressing the **Delete** key.

12.Graph the Duration of a Coupon Bond and Zero Coupon Bond. Highlight the range **B13:AE13** and then while holding down the **Ctrl** button highlight the range **B15:AE16**. Next choose **Insert Chart** from the main menu. Select an **XY(Scatter)** chart type and make other selections to complete the Chart Wizard. Place the graph in the range **E2:K11**.

Your *Dynamic Chart* allows you to change the Bond Duration inputs and instantly see the impact on a graph of the duration of a coupon bond and zero coupon bond by time to maturity. This allows you to perform instant experiments on Bond Duration. Below is a list of experiments that you might want to perform:

- What happens when the annual coupon rate is increased?

- What happens when the yield to maturity is increased?

- What happens when the number of payments / year is increased?

- What happens when the annual coupon rate is decreased to zero?

- What is the relationship between the duration of a zero coupon bond and time to maturity?

- Does an increase in the time to maturity always increase the duration of a coupon bond or is it possible for it to decrease duration at some point? Asked differently, does the red curve always go up or can it be hump shaped?

BOND DURATION
Problems

Problems To Build And Use The Spreadsheet Models

1. A bond has a face value of $1,000, an annual coupon rate of 3.70%, an yield to maturity of 7.4%, makes 2 (semi-annual) coupon payments per year, and 6 periods to maturity (or 3 years to maturity). Build the **Bond Duration - Basics** model and use it to determine the duration of this bond based on the Annual Percentage Rate (APR) convention and the duration of this bond based on the Effective Annual Rate (EAR) convention.

2. A bond has a face value of $1,000, an annual coupon rate of 6.50%, an yield to maturity of 9.2%, makes 2 (semi-annual) coupon payments per year, and 10 periods to maturity (or 5 years to maturity). Build the **Bond Duration - Price Sensitivity Using Duration** model and use it to approximate what percent change in bond price will result from a given change in yield to maturity and show the duration approximation on a graph and compared to the actual percent change in the bond price.

3. Build the **Bond Duration - Dynamic Chart** model and use it to perform instant experiments on whether changing various inputs causes an increase or decrease in the Bond Duration and by how much.

(a.) What happens when the annual coupon rate is increased?

(b.) What happens when the yield to maturity is increased?

(c.) What happens when the number of payments / year is increased?

(d.) What happens when the annual coupon rate is decreased to zero?

(e.) What is the relationship between the duration of a zero coupon bond and time to maturity?

(f.) Does an increase in the time to maturity always increase the duration of a coupon bond or is it possible for it to decrease duration at some point? Asked differently, does the duration curve always go up or can it be hump shaped?

BOND CONVEXITY
Basics

Problem. A bond has a face value of $1,000 , an annual coupon rate of 5.0% , an yield to maturity of 9.0% , makes 2 (semi-annual) coupon payments per year, and 8 periods to maturity (or 4 years to maturity). What is the convexity of this bond?

Solution Strategy. We will calculate convexity two equivalent ways. First, we will calculate convexity as the weighted-average (time-squared plus time) to the bond's cash flows. Second, we use a formula for convexity.

FIGURE 1. Spreadsheet Model of Bond Convexity - Basics.

	A	B	C	D	E	F	G	H	I	J	K
1	**BOND CONVEXITY**	**Basics**		**Annual Percentage Rate**							
2											
3	**Inputs**										
4	Rate Convention: 1 = EAR, 0 = APR	0									
5	Annual Coupon Rate (CR)	5.0%									
6	Yield to Maturity (Annualized) (y)	9.0%									
7	Number of Payments / Year (NOP)	2									
8	Number of Periods to Maturity (T)	8									
9	Face Value (FV)	$1,000									
10											
11	**Outputs**										
12	Discount Rate / Period (RATE)	4.5%									
13	Coupon Payment (PMT)	$25									
14											
15	**Calculate Bond Convexity using the Cash Flows**										
16	Period	0	1	2	3	4	5	6	7	8	
17	Time (Years)	0.0	0.5	1.0	1.5	2.0	2.5	3.0	3.5	4.0	Total
18	Cash Flows		$25.00	$25.00	$25.00	$25.00	$25.00	$25.00	$25.00	$1,025.00	
19	Present Value of Cash Flow		$23.92	$22.89	$21.91	$20.96	$20.06	$19.20	$18.37	$720.76	$868.08
20	Weight		2.8%	2.6%	2.5%	2.4%	2.3%	2.2%	2.1%	83.0%	100.0%
21	Weight * (Time^2+Time)		0.02	0.05	0.09	0.14	0.20	0.27	0.33	16.61	17.72
22	Convexity	16.23									
23											
24	**Calculate Bond Convexity using the Formula**										
25	Convexity	16.23									

How To Build This Spreadsheet Model.

1.Enter The Inputs and Name Them. Enter **0** in cell **B4**. This will serve as a switch between the APR and the EAR rate conventions. To highlight which rate convention is in use, enter **=IF ($B$4=1,"Effective Annual Rate","Annual Percentage Rate")** in cell **D1**. Enter the other inputs into the range **B5:B9** and then name each one. Put the cursor on cell **B5**, click on **Insert**, **Name**, **Define**, enter **CR** in the **Names in Workbook** box, and click on **OK**. Put the cursor on cell **B6** and repeat the process to name it **y**. Repeat the process to give the cells **B7**, **B8**, and **B9** the names **NOP**, **T**, and **FV**, respectively.

2.Calculate the Discount Rate / Period. The Discount Rate / Period depends on the rate convention being used as follows:

$$\text{Discount Rate / Period} = \begin{cases} (1+\text{Yield To Maturity})^{\wedge}(1/(\text{Number of Payments / Year}))-1 & \text{under EAR} \\ (\text{Yield To Maturity})/(\text{Number of Payments / Year}) & \text{under APR} \end{cases}$$

Enter **=IF($B$4=1,((1+y)^(1/NOP))-1,y/NOP)** in cell **B12** and use the process above to give the cell **B12** the name **RATE**.

3.Calculate the Coupon Payment. The formula is Coupon Payment = Coupon Rate * Face Value / (Number of Payments / Year). Enter **=CR*FV/NOP** in cell **B13** and use the process above to give the cell **B13** the name **PMT**.

4.Calculate Bond Convexity using the Cash Flows. Calculating duration as a weighted-average time to cash flows directly illustrates the key intuition for duration. This bond has two cash flows per year for four years or eight periods. Enter the period numbers **0, 1, 2, ..., 8** in the range **B16:J16**. Complete the duration calculation as follows:

- Time (years) = (Period) / (Number of Payments / Year) = Period / NOP. Enter **=B16/NOP** in cell **B17** and copy this cell to the range **C17:J17**.

- Cash Flows in Periods 1-7 = Coupon Payment. Enter **=PMT** in cell **C18** and copy this cell to the range **D18:J18**.

- Cash Flow in Period 8 = Coupon Payment + Face Value. Add **+FV** to the formula in cell **J18**, so that it reads **=PMT+FV**.

- Present Value of Cash Flow =(Cash Flow)/((1+Yield to Maturity/Number of Payments)^ Period) = Cash Flow / ((1+ y / NOP)^Period). Enter **=C18/((1+RATE)^C16)** in cell **C19** and copy this cell to the range **D19:J19**.

- Present Value of the Bond = Sum of all the Present Value of Cash Flows (row 14). Enter **=SUM(C19:J19)** in cell **K19**.

- Weight on date t = Present Value of Cash Flow on date t / Present Value of the Bond. Enter **=C19/$K$19** in cell **C20** and copy this cell to the range **D20:K20**.

- Weight * (Time^2 + Time). Enter **=C20*(C17^2+C17)**in cell **C21** and copy this cell to the range **D21:J21**.

- Convexity = (Sum of: Weight * (Time^2 + Time)) / ((1+Yield to Maturity / Number of Pmts) ^2). Enter **=SUM(C21:J21)/((1+y/NOP)^2)** in cell **B22**. Optionally for completeness, enter **=SUM(C21:J21)** in cell **K21**.

5.Calculate Bond Convexity by Formula. The calculation above can be simplified down to an equivalent formula solution for convexity. The convexity formula is

$$\frac{\left(\begin{array}{l} CR \cdot (1+RATE)^{1+T} \cdot \left(RATE \cdot (NOP+1)+2\right) \\ -CR \cdot \left(RATE^2 \cdot (NOP+T+1) \cdot (T+1) + RATE \cdot (NOP+2 \cdot T+3)+2\right) + RATE^3 \cdot NOP \cdot T \cdot (NOP+T) \end{array}\right)}{RATE^2 \cdot NOP^2 \cdot \left(CR \cdot (1+RATE)^T - CR + RATE \cdot NOP\right)}$$
$$\div \left((1+RATE)^2\right)$$

Enter **= ((CR*((1+RATE)^(1+T))*(RATE*(NOP+1)+2)CR*(RATE^2*(NOP+T+1)*(T+1)+RATE* (NOP+2*T+3)+2)+RATE^3*NOP*T*(NOP+T))/(RATE^2*NOP^2*(CR*(1+RATE)^T-CR+RATE* NOP))) / ((1+RATE)^2)** in cell **B25**.

The value of bond convexity is 16.23. Notice you get the same answer both ways: using the cash flows or using the formula!

BOND CONVEXITY
Price Sensitivity Including Convexity

Bond convexity complements bond duration in measuring of the price sensitivity of a bond to changes in interest rates. In other words, duration and convexity combined give you a measure of the bond's interest rate risk. Adding convexity gives you a better approximation of what percent change in bond price will result from a given change in yield to maturity than you can get from duration alone. To get the overall picture we will compare all three on a graph: the duration approximation, the duration and convexity approximation, and the actual percent change in the bond price.

FIGURE 1. Spreadsheet Model of Bond Convexity - Price Sensitivity Including Convexity.

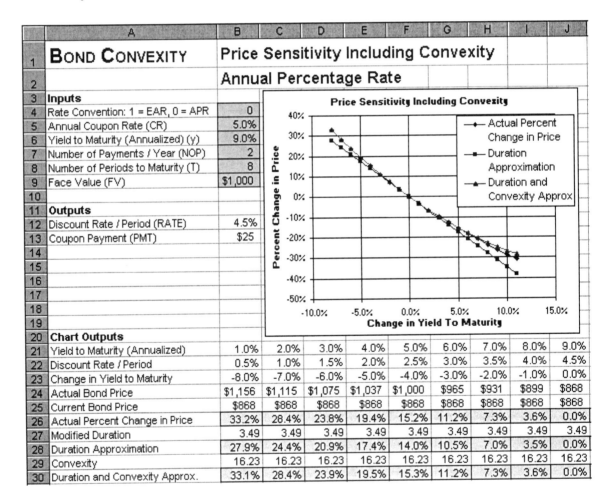

	A	B	C	D	E	F	G	H	I	J
1	**BOND CONVEXITY**	**Price Sensitivity Including Convexity**								
2		**Annual Percentage Rate**								
3	**Inputs**									
4	Rate Convention: 1 = EAR, 0 = APR	0								
5	Annual Coupon Rate (CR)	5.0%								
6	Yield to Maturity (Annualized) (y)	9.0%								
7	Number of Payments / Year (NOP)	2								
8	Number of Periods to Maturity (T)	8								
9	Face Value (FV)	$1,000								
10										
11	**Outputs**									
12	Discount Rate / Period (RATE)	4.5%								
13	Coupon Payment (PMT)	$25								
14										
15										
16										
17										
18										
19										
20	**Chart Outputs**									
21	Yield to Maturity (Annualized)	1.0%	2.0%	3.0%	4.0%	5.0%	6.0%	7.0%	8.0%	9.0%
22	Discount Rate / Period	0.5%	1.0%	1.5%	2.0%	2.5%	3.0%	3.5%	4.0%	4.5%
23	Change in Yield to Maturity	-8.0%	-7.0%	-6.0%	-5.0%	-4.0%	-3.0%	-2.0%	-1.0%	0.0%
24	Actual Bond Price	$1,156	$1,115	$1,075	$1,037	$1,000	$965	$931	$899	$868
25	Current Bond Price	$868	$868	$868	$868	$868	$868	$868	$868	$868
26	Actual Percent Change in Price	33.2%	28.4%	23.8%	19.4%	15.2%	11.2%	7.3%	3.6%	0.0%
27	Modified Duration	3.49	3.49	3.49	3.49	3.49	3.49	3.49	3.49	3.49
28	Duration Approximation	27.9%	24.4%	20.9%	17.4%	14.0%	10.5%	7.0%	3.5%	0.0%
29	Convexity	16.23	16.23	16.23	16.23	16.23	16.23	16.23	16.23	16.23
30	Duration and Convexity Approx.	33.1%	28.4%	23.9%	19.5%	15.3%	11.2%	7.3%	3.6%	0.0%

How To Build This Spreadsheet Model.

1.Start with the Basics Spreadsheet and Delete Rows. Open the spreadsheet that you created for Bond Convexity - Basics and immediately save the spreadsheet under a new name using the **File Save As** command. Delete rows **14** through **24** by selecting the range **A14:A24**, clicking on **Edit**, **Delete**, selecting the **Entire Row** radio button on the **Delete** dialog box, and clicking on **OK**. Do not delete row 25 at this time, since later we want to copy the convexity formula rather than reenter it!

2.Yield To Maturity (Annualized). Enter Yield To Maturity values **1.0%**, **2.0%**, **3.0%**, **4.0%**, **...**, **20.0%** in the range **B21:U21**.

3.Discount Rate / Period. The Discount Rate / Period depends on the rate convention being used as follows:

$$\text{Discount Rate / Period} = \begin{cases} (1 + \text{Yield To Maturity})^{\wedge}(1/(\text{Number of Payments / Year})) - 1 & \text{under EAR} \\ (\text{Yield To Maturity})/(\text{Number of Payments / Year}) & \text{under APR} \end{cases}$$

Enter **=IF($B$4=1,((1+B21)^(1/NOP))-1,B21/NOP)** in cell **B22** and copy the cell **B22** to the range **C22:U22**.

4.Change in Yield To Maturity. The Change in Yield To Maturity = New Yield To Maturity - Current Yield To Maturity (y). In cell **B23**, enter **=B21-y** and copy the cell **B23** to the range **C23:U23**.

5.Actual Bond Price. Calculate the bond price using the inputs **T, PMT, FV**, and the Discount Rate / Period in cell **B22**. Specifically, enter **=-PV(B22,T,PMT,FV)** in cell **B24** and copy the cell **B24** to the range **C24:U24**.

6.Current Bond Price. Calculate the bond price using the original inputs. Copy the formula in cell **B24** to cell **B25**. Then change the yield to maturity from **B23** to **RATE** so that the formula reads **=-PV(RATE,T,PMT,FV)** and copy the cell **B25** to the range **C25:U25**.

7.Actual Percent Change in Price. The percent Actual Percent Change in Price = (Actual Bond Price -Current Bond Price) / Current Bond Price. In cell **B26**, enter **=(B24-B25)/B25** and copy the cell **B26** to the range **C26:U26**.

8.Modified Duration. Enter the modified duration formula **=((1+RATE)/(RATE*NOP)- (1+RATE+T*(CR/NOP-RATE)) / (CR*((1+RATE)^T-1)+RATE*NOP)) / (1+RATE)** in cell **B27** to the range **C27:U27**.

9.Duration Approximation. The Duration Approximation of the Percent Change in Price = - Modified Duration * Change in Yield To Maturity. In cell **B28**, enter **=-B27*B23** and copy the cell **B28** to the range **C28:U28**.

10.Convexity. Copy the convexity formula in cell **B14** to cell **B29** and copy the cell **B29** to the range **C29:U29**. For appearances, delete the range **A14:B14**.

11.Duration and Convexity Approx. The Duration and Convexity Approximation = Duration Approximation + (1/2) * Convexity * (Change in Yield To Maturity)^2. In cell **B30**, enter **=B28+ (1/2)*B29*B23^2** and copy the cell **B30** to the range **C30:U30**.

12.Graph the Actual Percent Change in Price and the Duration Approximation. Highlight the range **A23:U23** and then while holding down the **Ctrl** button highlight the ranges **A26:U26**, **A28:U28**, and **A30:U30**. Next choose **Insert Chart** from the main menu. Select an **XY(Scatter)** chart type and make other selections to complete the Chart Wizard. Place the graph in the range **C3:J20**.

The graph illustrates that duration and convexity approximation of the price sensitivity of a bond is better than the duration approximation alone. That is, the percent change in bond price from the duration and convexity approximation is very close to the actual percent change over a wide range of changes in yield to maturity (say, plus or minus 9%). Only for very large changes in yield to maturity is there any gap between the duration and convexity approximation and the actual percent change and the gap is pretty small. In approximating the actual percent change, duration alone does a good job of approximating the slope. Then convexity does a good job of adding the curvature. Together they do a great job of approximating the price sensitivity (i.e., interest rate risk) of a bond over a wide range of changes in yields.

BOND CONVEXITY
Dynamic Chart

If you increased the coupon rate of a bond, what would happen to it's convexity? If you increased the yield to maturity of a bond, what would happen to it's convexity? You can answer these questions and more by creating an *Dynamic Chart* using "spinners." Spinners are up-arrow / down-arrow buttons that allow you to easily change the inputs to the model with the click of a mouse. Then the spreadsheet recalculates the model and instantly redraws the model outputs on the graph.

FIGURE 1. Spreadsheet Model of Bond Convexity - Dynamic Chart.

	A	B	C	D	E	F	G	H	I	J	K
1	**BOND CONVEXITY**	**Dynamic Chart**				**Annual Percentage Rate**					
3	**Inputs**										
4	Rate Convention: 1 = EAR, 0 = APR	0	▲ ▼	0							
5	Annual Coupon Rate (CR)	5.0%	▲ ▼	10							
6	Yield to Maturity (Annualized) (y)	9.0%	▲ ▼	18							
7	Number of Payments / Year (NOP)	2	▲ ▼	2							
9	**Outputs**										
10	Discount Rate / Period (RATE)	4.5%									
12	**Dynamic Chart Outputs**										
13	Time to Maturity (Years)	1	2	3	4	5	6	7	8	9	10
14	Number of Periods to Maturity	2	4	6	8	10	12	14	16	18	20
15	Convexity of Coupon Bond	1.80	5.23	10.10	16.23	23.43	31.53	40.37	49.78	59.62	69.75
16	Convexity of Zero-Coupon Bond	1.83	5.49	10.99	18.31	27.47	38.46	51.28	65.93	82.42	100.73

How To Build This Spreadsheet Model.

1. Start with the Basics Spreadsheet and Delete Rows. Open the spreadsheet that you created for Bond Convexity - Basics and immediately save the spreadsheet under a new name using the **File Save As** command. Delete rows **13** through **24** by selecting the range **A13:A24**, clicking on **Edit, Delete**, selecting the **Entire Row** radio button on the **Delete** dialog box, and clicking on **OK** Repeat this procedure to delete rows **9** through **10**.

2.Increase Row Height for the Spinners. Select the range **A4:A7**. Then click on **Format Row Height** from the main menu. Enter a height of **30** and click on **OK**.

3.Display the Forms Toolbar. Click on **View**, **Toolbars**, **Forms** from the main menu.

4.Create the Spinners. Look for the up-arrow / down-arrow button on the **Forms** toolbar (which will display the word "**Spinner**" if you hover the cursor over it) and click on it. Then draw the box for a spinner from the upper left corner of cell **C4** down to the lower right corner of the cell. Then a spinner appears in the cell **C4**. Right click on the spinner (press the right mouse button while the cursor is above the spinner) and a small menu pops up. Click on **Copy**. Then select the cell **C5** and click on **Paste**. This creates an identical spinner in the cell **C5**. Repeat the process twice more. Select cell **C6** and click on **Paste**. Select cell **C6** and click on **Paste**. You now have four spinners down column **C**.

5.Create The Cell Links. Right click on the first spinner in the cell **C4** and a small menu pops up. Click on **Format Control** and a dialog box pops up. Click on the **Control** tab, then enter the cell link **D4** in the **Cell link** edit box and click on **OK**. Repeat this procedure for the other three spinners. Link the spinner in cell **C5** to cell **D5**. Link the spinner in cell **C6** to cell **D6**. Link the spinner in cell **C7** to cell **D7** and also on the **Control tab**, set the **Minimum value** equal to **1**. Test your spinners by clicking on the up-arrows and down-arrows of the spinners to see how they change the values in the linked cells.

6.Create Scaled Inputs. The values in the linked cells are always integers, but they can be scaled appropriately to the problem at hand. Restrict the value in cell **B4** to be either 1 or 0 by entering **=IF(D4>1,1,D4)**. In cell **B5**, enter **=D5/200**. In cell **B6**, enter **=D6/200**. In cell **B7**, enter **=D7**.

7.Time To Maturity. Enter Time To Maturity values **1, 2, 3, 4, ..., 30** in the range **B13:AE13**.

8.Number of Periods to Maturity. The Number of Periods to Maturity = (Time to Maturity) * (Number of Periods / Year). In cell **B14**, enter **=B13*NOP** and copy the cell **B14** to the range **C14:AE14**.

9.Convexity of a Coupon Bond. Copy the convexity formula in cell **B11** to cell **B15**. Then edit the formula in cell **B15** so as to change every occurrence of the variable **T** to **B$14** (with a $ in the middle to lock in the row, but not the column). You will find 7 occurrences of the variable **T** to change. Copy the cell **B15** to the range **C15:AE15**. For appearances, delete the range **A11:B11**.

10.Convexity of a Zero Coupon Bond. A zero coupon bond is a bond with a coupon rate equal to 0.0%. As a benchmark for comparison, calculate the duration of a zero-coupon bond using the same inputs for everything else. Copy the formula in cell **B15** to cell **B16**. Then edit the formula in cell **B16** so as to change every occurrence of the variable **CR** to **0**. You will find 4 occurrences of the variable **CR** to change. Copy the cell **B16** to the range **C16:AE16**.

11.Graph the Convexity of a Coupon Bond and Zero Coupon Bond. Highlight the range **B13:AE13** and then while holding down the **Ctrl** button highlight the range **B15:AE16**. Next choose **Insert Chart** from the main menu. Select an **XY(Scatter)** chart type and make other selections to complete the Chart Wizard. Place the graph in the range **E2:K11**.

Your *Dynamic Chart* allows you to change the Bond Convexity inputs and instantly see the impact on a graph of the convexity of a coupon bond and zero coupon bond by time to maturity. This allows you to perform instant experiments on Bond Convexity. Below is a list of experiments that you might want to perform:

- What happens when the annual coupon rate is increased?

- What happens when the yield to maturity is increased?

- What happens when the number of payments / year is increased?

- What happens when the annual coupon rate is decreased to zero?

- Does an increase in the time to maturity *always* increase the convexity of a coupon bond or is it possible for it to decrease convexity at some point? Asked differently, does the red curve always go up or can it be hump shaped?

BOND CONVEXITY
Problems

Problems To Build And Use The Spreadsheet Models

1. A bond has a face value of $1,000, an annual coupon rate of 2.30%, an yield to maturity of 8.9%, makes 2 (semi-annual) coupon payments per year, and 10 periods to maturity (or 5 years to maturity). Build the **Bond Convexity - Basics** model and use it to determine the convexity of this bond based on the Annual Percentage Rate (APR) convention and the convexity of this bond based on the Effective Annual Rate (EAR) convention.

2. A bond has a face value of $1,000, an annual coupon rate of 4.70%, an yield to maturity of 7.8%, makes 2 (semi-annual) coupon payments per year, and 8 periods to maturity (or 4 years to maturity). Build the **Bond Convexity - Price Sensitivity Using Duration And Convexity** model and use it to approximate what percent change in bond price will result from a given change in yield to maturity and compare on a graph the duration approximation, the duration and convexity approximation, and the actual percent change in the bond price.

3. Build the **Bond Convexity - Dynamic Chart** model and use it to perform instant experiments on whether changing various inputs causes an increase or decrease in the Bond Convexity and by how much.

(a.) What happens when the annual coupon rate is increased?

(b.) What happens when the yield to maturity is increased?

(c.) What happens when the number of payments / year is increased?

(d.) What happens when the annual coupon rate is decreased to zero?

(e.) Does an increase in the time to maturity always increase the convexity of a coupon bond or is it possible for it to decrease convexity at some point? Asked differently, does the convexity curve always go up or can it be hump shaped?

US YIELD CURVE DYNAMICS
Dynamic Chart

How does the US yield curve change over time? What determines the volatility of changes in the yield curve? Are there differences in the volatility of short rates, medium rates, long rates, etc.? You can answer these questions and more using a *Dynamic Chart* of the yield curve, which is based on 30 years of monthly US zero-coupon, yield curve data.

I have made a major exception for this spreadsheet model and provided the model already built. To load the model, click on US Yield Curve Dynamics - Dynamic Chart.xls. I will update this spreadsheet model each month with the latest yield curve data and make it available for free in the "Free Samples" section of spreadsheetmodeling.com.

The step-by-step instructions below explain how it you can build this model. The dynamic chart uses "spinners," which are up-arrow / down-arrow buttons, that allow you to advance the yield curve graph from month to month. This allows you to see a dynamic "movie" or animation of the yield curve over time. Thus, you can directly observe the volatility of the yield curve and other dynamic properties For details of what to look for, see the discussion below on "using the spreadsheet model."

FIGURE 1. Spreadsheet Model of US Yield Curve Dynamics - Dynamic Chart.

How To Build This Spreadsheet Model.

1.Start with a Spreadsheet Containing the Yield Curve Database. Click on US Yield Curve Dynamics - Database.xls to open a spreadsheet containing the yield curve database (see Figure 2). Columns **A**, **B**, and **C** contain three sets of titles for the dataset. Columns **D**, **E**, and **F** contain yield data for bond maturities of one month, three months, and six months (0.833, 0.25, and 0.50 years, respectively). Columns **G** through **P** contain yield data for bond maturities of 1, 2, 3, 4, 5, 10, 15, 20, 25, and 30 years. Rows **2** through **9** contain examples of static features yield curve that can be observed from actual data in a particular month. For example, the yield curve is sometimes upward sloping (as it was in Nov 87) or downward sloping (in Nov 80) or flat (in Jan 70) or hump shaped (in Dec 78). Rows **10** through **375** contain monthly US zero-coupon, yield curve data from January 1970 through June 2000. For the period from January 1970 through December 1991, the database is based on the Bliss (1992) monthly estimates of the zero-coupon, yield curve. Bliss fits a parsimonious, nonlinear function that is capable of matching all of the empirically observed shapes of the zero-coupon, yield curve. For more details see Bliss, R., 1992, "Testing Term Structure Estimation Methods," Indiana University Discussion Paper #519. For the period from January 1992 to June 2000, the yield curve is directly observed from Treasury Bills and Strips in the *Wall Street Journal*.

FIGURE 2. Spreadsheet Containing the Yield Curve Database.

	A	B	C	D	E	F	G	H	I
1	Title 1	Title 2	Title 3	0.0833	0.25	0.5	1	2	3
2	Static Features:	Shape = Upward	Nov-87	3.65%	5.36%	6.43%	7.09%	7.64%	8.04%
3	Static Features:	Shape = Downward	Nov-80	14.83%	14.60%	14.64%	14.17%	13.22%	12.75%
4	Static Features:	Shape = Flat	Jan-70	7.73%	8.00%	8.03%	7.98%	7.95%	7.94%
5	Static Features:	Shape = Hump	Dec-78	8.82%	9.48%	9.99%	10.18%	9.76%	9.40%
6	Static Features:	Level = Low	Dec-70	4.62%	4.91%	4.95%	5.02%	5.40%	5.69%
7	Static Features:	Level = High	Oct-81	12.65%	13.13%	13.53%	13.85%	14.01%	14.06%
8	Static Features:	Curvature = Little	Dec-72	4.93%	5.24%	5.44%	5.62%	5.86%	6.01%
9	Static Features:	Curvature = Lot	Sep-82	6.67%	7.87%	9.05%	10.29%	11.16%	11.43%
10	Monthly Dynamics:		Jan-70	7.73%	8.00%	8.03%	7.98%	7.95%	7.94%
11	Monthly Dynamics:		Feb-70	6.23%	6.99%	6.97%	6.96%	7.02%	7.04%
12	Monthly Dynamics:		Mar-70	6.33%	6.44%	6.53%	6.67%	6.85%	6.95%
13	Monthly Dynamics:		Apr-70	6.48%	7.03%	7.35%	7.50%	7.60%	7.67%
14	Monthly Dynamics:		May-70	6.22%	7.03%	7.28%	7.45%	7.58%	7.63%
15	Monthly Dynamics:		Jun-70	6.14%	6.47%	6.81%	7.17%	7.43%	7.53%
16	Monthly Dynamics:		Jul-70	6.32%	6.38%	6.55%	6.87%	7.19%	7.31%
17	Monthly Dynamics:		Aug-70	6.22%	6.38%	6.57%	6.83%	7.07%	7.18%
18	Monthly Dynamics:		Sep-70	5.32%	6.04%	6.49%	6.63%	6.64%	6.77%
19	Monthly Dynamics:		Oct-70	5.23%	5.91%	6.23%	6.33%	6.50%	6.69%
20	Monthly Dynamics:		Nov-70	4.86%	5.05%	5.11%	5.10%	5.29%	5.59%
21	Monthly Dynamics:		Dec-70	4.62%	4.91%	4.95%	5.02%	5.40%	5.69%

2.Create a Spinner. Click on **View**, **Toolbars**, **Forms** from the main menu. Look for the up-arrow / down-arrow button on the **Forms** toolbar (which will display the word **"Spinner"** if you hover the cursor over it) and click on it. Then draw the box for a spinner in the range **R4:R5**.

3.Create The Cell Link. Right click on the spinner and a small menu pops up. Click on **Format Control** and a dialog box pops up. Click on the **Control** tab, then enter the cell link **R6** in the **Cell link** edit box, set the **Minimum value** equal to **2**, and click on **OK**. Test your spinner by clicking on the up-arrows and down-arrows of the spinner to see how it changes the value in the linked cell.

4.Time To Maturity. Reference the Database's Time To Maturity valuesÊin the range **D1:P1**, by entering **=D1** in cell **S21** and copying the cell to the range **T21:AE21**.

5.Yield To Maturity. Reference the Database's Yield To Maturity values using the Excel **HLOOKUP** function. The format is =HLOOKUP(Lookup value, Database, Row). The Lookup value is the corresponding Time To Maturity, the database is the range **A1:P600**, which has already been given the range name "**Database**," and the Row is the linked cell **R6**. Enter **=HLOOKUP(S21,Database,$R$6)** in cell **S22** and copy the cell to the range **T22:AF22**.

6.Graph the Yield To Maturity by Time To Maturity. Highlight the range **S21:AE22**. Next choose **Insert Chart** from the main menu. Select an **XY(Scatter)** chart type and make other selections to complete the Chart Wizard. Place the graph in the range **S3:Z20**.

7.Three Titles. Reference the Database's three columns of Title values using the Excel **HLOOKUP** function. The format is same as above, except that the Lookup value will be the column headings ("Title 1", etc.) that we wish to reference. Enter **=HLOOKUP("Title 1",Database,$R$6)** in cell **S2**, **=HLOOKUP("Title 2",Database,$R$6)** in cell **V2**, and **=HLOOKUP("Title 3",Database,$R$6)** in cell **Z2**. To format the date title, select cell **Z2**, click on **Format Cells**, click on **Date** in the Category list box, click on **Mar-98** format in the Type list box, and click on **OK**.

Using The Spreadsheet Model.

To run the Dynamic Chart, click on the up arrow of the spinner. The movie / animation begins with some background on the yield curve's static features. In the 30 year database we observe:

- four different **shapes**: upward-sloping, downward-sloping, flat, and hump-shaped,

- the overall **level** of the yield curve ranges from low to high, and

- the amount of **curvature** at the short end ranges from a little to a lot.

Keep clicking on the spinner and you will get to the section of the Dynamic Chart covering 30 years of the US yield curve history. This section shows the yield curve on a month by month basis. For example, Figure 3 shows the US yield curve in November 1970.

FIGURE 3. Spreadsheet Containing the Month By Month History - Dynamic Chart.

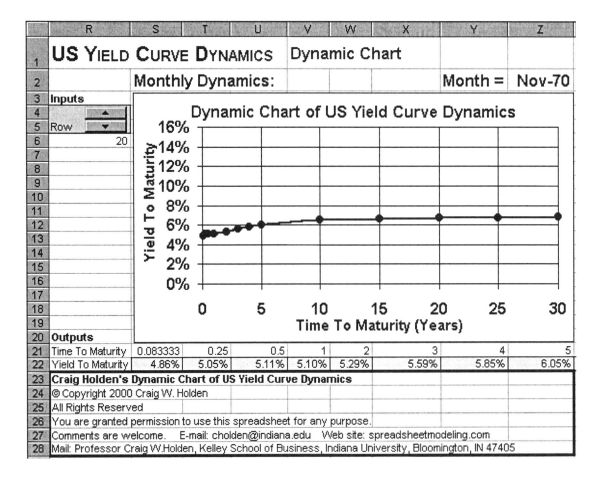

	R	S	T	U	V	W	X	Y	Z
1	US YIELD CURVE DYNAMICS			Dynamic Chart					
2		Monthly Dynamics:						Month =	Nov-70
3	Inputs								
4	▲								
5	Row ▼								
6	20								
20	Outputs								
21	Time To Maturity	0.083333	0.25	0.5	1	2	3	4	5
22	Yield To Maturity	4.86%	5.05%	5.11%	5.10%	5.29%	5.59%	5.85%	6.05%
23	Craig Holden's Dynamic Chart of US Yield Curve Dynamics								
24	© Copyright 2000 Craig W. Holden								
25	All Rights Reserved								
26	You are granted permission to use this spreadsheet for any purpose.								
27	Comments are welcome. E-mail: cholden@indiana.edu Web site: spreadsheetmodeling.com								
28	Mail: Professor Craig W.Holden, Kelley School of Business, Indiana University, Bloomington, IN 47405								

Keep clicking on the spinner and you will see the yield curve move around over time. By observing this movie / animation, you should be able to recognize the following key **dynamic** properties of the yield curve:

- short rates (the 0 to 5 year piece of the yield curve) are more volatile than long rates (the 15 to 30 year piece),

- the overall volatility of the yield curve is higher when the level is higher (especially in the early 80's), and

- sometimes there are sharp reactions to government intervention.

As an example of the later, consider what happened in 1980. Figure 4 shows the yield curve in January 1980.

FIGURE 4. Spreadsheet Showing The Yield Curve in January 1980.

	R	S	T	U	V	W	X	Y	Z
1	US YIELD CURVE DYNAMICS				Dynamic Chart				
2		Monthly Dynamics:						Month =	Jan-80
3	Inputs								
4	▲								
5	Row ▼								
6	130								
20	Outputs								
21	Time To Maturity	0.083333	0.25	0.5	1	2	3	4	5
22	Yield To Maturity	11.69%	12.42%	12.31%	11.68%	11.16%	10.98%	10.89%	10.83%
23	Craig Holden's Dynamic Chart of US Yield Curve Dynamics								
24	© Copyright 2000 Craig W. Holden								
25	All Rights Reserved								
26	You are granted permission to use this spreadsheet for any purpose.								
27	Comments are welcome. E-mail: cholden@indiana.edu Web site: spreadsheetmodeling.com								
28	Mail: Professor Craig W.Holden, Kelley School of Business, Indiana University, Bloomington, IN 47405								

Rows 4 through 19 contain the chart:

Dynamic Chart of US Yield Curve Dynamics

Yield To Maturity (vertical axis): 0% to 16%
Time To Maturity (Years) (horizontal axis): 0 to 30

Short rates were around 12% and long rates were at 10.7%. President Jimmy Carter was running for re-election. He wished to manipulate the election year economy to make it better for his re-election bid. His strategy for doing this was to impose credit controls on the banking system. Click on the spinner to see what the reaction of the financial market was.

FIGURE 5. Spreadsheet Showing The Yield Curve in March 1980.

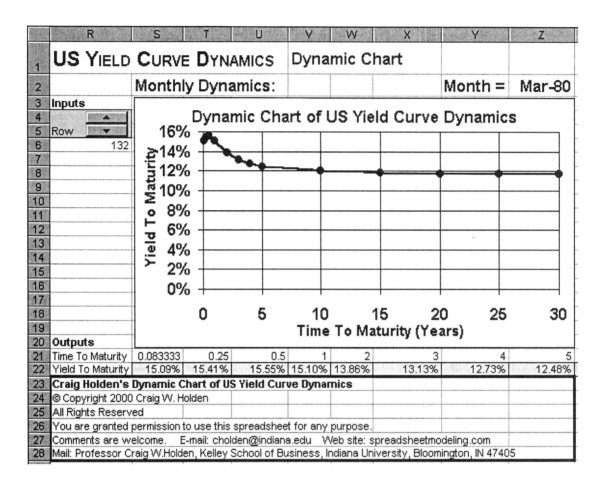

In two months time, the short rate when up to 15.5%, an increase of 3.5%! What a disaster! This was the opposite of the reaction the Carter had intended. Notice that long rates when up to 11.7%, an increase of only 1%. Apparently, the market expected that this intervention would only be a short-lived phenomena. Carter quickly realized what a big political mistake he had made and announced that the credit controls were being dropped. Click on the spinner to see what the reaction of the financial market was.

FIGURE 6. Spreadsheet Showing The Yield Curve in April 1980.

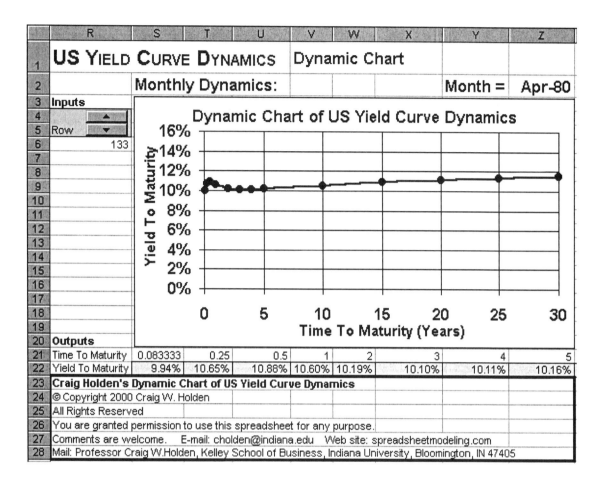

Short rates dropped to 10.9%! A drop of 4.6% in one month! The high interest rates went away, but the political damage was done. This is the single biggest change in the yield curve in 30 years.

PORTFOLIO OPTIMIZATION
Two Assets

Problem. The riskless rate is 6.0%. Risky Asset 1 has a mean return of 14.0% and a standard deviation of 20.0%. Risky Asset 2 has a mean return of 8.0% and a standard deviation of 15.0% The correlation between Risky Asset 1 and 2 is 0.0%. Graph the Efficient Trade-Off Line and the Risky Asset Trade-Off Curve.

Solution Strategy. Determine the Risky Asset Trade-Off Curve for two-asset portfolios by varying the proportion in the first asset and calculating the resulting portfolio's standard deviation and expected return. Then, determine the Optimal Combination of Risky Assets by calculating the optimal proportion in the first asset and calculating the corresponding standard deviation and expected return. Finally, determine the Efficient Trade-Off Line by varying the amount in the Optimal Combination and calculating the corresponding standard deviation and expected return. Then graph everything.

FIGURE 1. Spreadsheet for Portfolio Optimization - Two Assets

How To Build Your Own Spreadsheet Model.

1.Inputs. Enter the inputs described above into the ranges **B5:B7** and **C6:C8**.

2.Expected Return - Riskless Rate. Calculate the Expected Return minus the Riskless Rate by entering **=B5-$B$5** in cell **D5** and copying that cell to the range **D6:D7**.

FIGURE 2. Spreadsheet Details for Portfolio Optimization - Two Assets

	A	B	C	D	E
18	Outputs			Risk - Ret	Efficient
19		Proportion		Trade-off	Trade-off
20		in Risky	(x-axis)	Curve	Line
21		Asset 1 or	Standard	Expected	Expected
22		Opt Comb	Deviation	Return	Return
23	Trade-off Curve	-60.0%	26.8%	4.4%	
24	Trade-off Curve	-50.0%	24.6%	5.0%	
25	Trade-off Curve	-40.0%	22.5%	5.6%	
26	Trade-off Curve	-30.0%	20.4%	6.2%	
27	Trade-off Curve	-20.0%	18.4%	6.8%	
28	Trade-off Curve	-10.0%	16.6%	7.4%	
29	Trade-off Curve	0.0%	15.0%	8.0%	
30	Trade-off Curve	10.0%	13.6%	8.6%	
31	Trade-off Curve	20.0%	12.6%	9.2%	
32	Trade-off Curve	30.0%	12.1%	9.8%	
33	Trade-off Curve	40.0%	12.0%	10.4%	
34	Trade-off Curve	50.0%	12.5%	11.0%	
35	Trade-off Curve	60.0%	13.4%	11.6%	
36	Trade-off Curve	70.0%	14.7%	12.2%	
37	Trade-off Curve	80.0%	16.3%	12.8%	
38	Trade-off Curve	90.0%	18.1%	13.4%	
39	Trade-off Curve	100.0%	20.0%	14.0%	
40	Trade-off Curve	110.0%	22.1%	14.6%	
41	Trade-off Curve	120.0%	24.2%	15.2%	
42	Trade-off Curve	130.0%	26.4%	15.8%	
43	Trade-off Curve	140.0%	28.6%	16.4%	
44	Optimal Comb.	69.2%	14.6%		12.2%
45	Eff Trade-off Lin	0.0%	0.0%		6.0%
46	Eff Trade-off Lin	100.0%	14.6%		12.2%
47	Eff Trade-off Lin	200.0%	29.2%		18.3%

3.Proportion in Risky Asset 1. In order graph the Risky Asset Trade-off Curve, we need to evaluate a wide range of values (-60.0% to 140%) for the Proportion in Risky Asset 1. Enter **-60.0%** in cell **B23**, **-50.0%** in cell **B24**, and highlight the range **B23:B24**. Then hover the cursor over the lower right corner and it turns to a "fill handle" (which looks like a "+" sign). Drag the fill handle down to **B43**.

4.Standard Deviation. The x-axis of our graph is the portfolio's standard deviation, which is calculated by the formula:

$$\sigma = \sqrt{w^2\sigma_1^2 + (1-w)^2\,\sigma_2^2 + 2w(1-w)\rho\sigma_1\sigma_2}$$

Enter **=SQRT(B23^2*$C$6^2+ (1-B23)^2*$C$7^2+2*B23* (1-B23) *$C$8*$C$6*$C$7)** in cell **C23** and copy the cell to the range **C24:C43**.

5.Expected Return. The formula for a portfolio's expected return is:

$$E(r) = wE(r_1) + (1-w)E(r_2)$$

Enter **=B23*$B$6+(1-B23)*$B$7** in cell **D23** and copy the cell to the range **D24:D43**.

6.Optimal Combination of Risky Assets. Using the notation that $E_1 = E(r_1) - r_f$ and $E_2 = E(r_2) - r_f$, then the formula for the optimal proportion in the first asset is:

$$w_1 = \left(E_1\sigma_2^2 - E_2\rho\sigma_1\sigma_2\right) / \left(E_1\sigma_2^2 + E_2\sigma_1^2 - \left(E_1 + E_2\right)\rho\sigma_1\sigma_2\right)$$

In cell **B44**, enter **=(D6*C7^2-D7*C8*C6*C7) / (D6*C7^2+D7*C6^2-(D6+D7)*C8*C6*C7)**. Calculate the corresponding Mean and Standard Deviation by copying the range **C43:D43** to the range **C44:D44**. We want to create a separate column for the Efficient Trade-Off Line, so move the formula in cell **D44** to cell **E44**. To do this, select cell **D44**, click on **Edit Cut**, select cell **E44**, and click on **Edit Paste**.

7.Efficient Trade-Off Line. The Efficient Trade-Off Line is a combination of the Riskless Asset and the Risky Asset Optimal Combination. It can be calculated as follows:

- Enter **0.0%** in cell **B45**, **100.0%** in cell **B46**, and **200.0%** in cell **B47**.
- Since the Riskless Asset has a standard deviation of zero, the standard deviation formula simplifies to $\sigma = w\sigma_T$, where σ_T = standard deviation of the Optimal Combination of Risky Assets (or Tangent Portfolio). Enter **=B45*$C$44** in cell **C45** and copy the cell to the range **C46:C47**.
- The Expected Return formula is $E(r) = E(r_T)w + r_f(1-w)$, were $E(r_T) =$ expected return of the Tangent Portfolio. Enter **=$E$44*B45+$B$5*(1-B45)** in cell **E45** and copy to the range **E46:E47**.

8.Create The Graph. Highlight the range **C23:E47** and then choose **Insert Chart** from the main menu. Select an **XY(Scatter)** chart type and make other selections to complete the Chart Wizard. Place the graph in the range **E2:J16**.

9.(Optional) Formatting The Graph. Here are some tips to make the chart look attractive:

- Click on one of the Chart curves, then click on **Format Selected Data Series**. In the Format Data Series dialog box under the **Patterns** tab, select **None** for the Marker and click on **OK**. Repeat for the other curve.

- Highlight individual points, such as the Riskless Asset, Tangent Portfolio, and Risky Assets 1 and 2, by clicking on a chart curve, then click a second time on an individual point (the four-way arrows symbol appears), then click on **Format Selected Data Point**. In the Format Data Point dialog box under the **Patterns** tab under the Marker, select a market Style, Foreground Color, Background Color, and increase the size to **8** pts and click on **OK**.

- Click on the x-axis, then click on **Format Selected Axis**. In the Format Axis dialog box under the **Scale** tab, enter **0.25** for the Maximum and click on **OK**.

Investors prefer points on the graph that yield higher mean returns (further "North") and lower standard deviations (further "West"). The graph shows that best combinations of high return and low risk (furthest in the "Northwest" direction) are given by the Efficient Trade-Off Line. Better combinations are simply not feasible. Since the Efficient Trade-Off Line is a combination of the Riskless Asset and a Tangent Portfolio, then all investors prefer to invest *only* in the Riskless Asset and a Tangent Portfolio.

PORTFOLIO OPTIMIZATION
Many Assets

Suppose that you had N risky assets, rather than just two risky assets. How would you calculate the Efficient Trade-Off Line and the Risky Asset Trade-Off Curve in this case? It turns out that it is much easier to handle N risky assets in a spreadsheet than any other way. The figure below shows the results of the N=5 risky assets case, including a bar chart of the portfolio weights of the optimal (tangent) portfolio.

FIGURE 1. Spreadsheet for Portfolio Optimization - Many Assets.

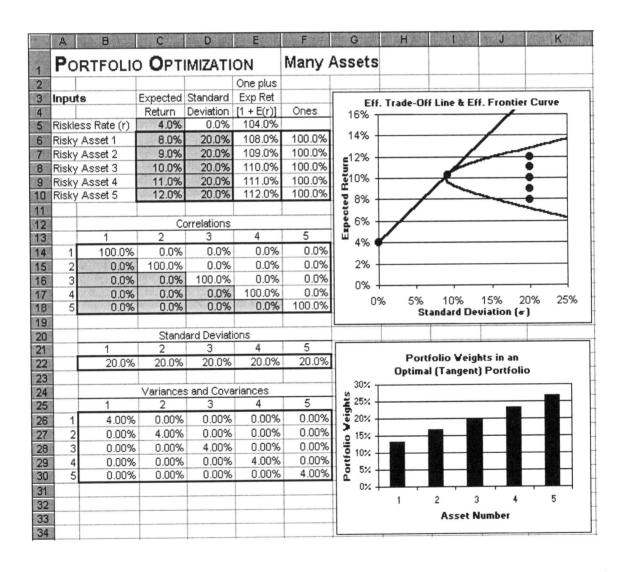

How To Build This Spreadsheet Model.

1.Inputs. Enter the expected return inputs into the range **C5:C10**, the standard deviation inputs into the range **D6:B10**, the correlation inputs in the triangular range from **B15** to **B18** to **E18**, and 0.0% in the cell **D5**.

2.One plus the Expected Return and 100%. It will be useful to have a column based on one plus the expected return and another column with just the number 100%. Enter **=1+C5** in cell **E5** and copy the cell to the range **E6:E10**. Enter **100%** in cell **F6** and copy the cell to the range **F7:F10**.

3.Fill Out the Correlations Table (Matrix). The correlations table (matrix) from **B14:F18** has a simple structure. All of the elements on the diagonal represent the correlation of an asset return with itself. For example, **B14** is the correlation of the Asset 1 return with the Asset 1 return, which is one. **C15** is the correlation of Asset 2 with 2, and so on. Enter **100.0%** into the diagonal cells from **B14** to **F18**. The off-diagonal cells in the *upper* triangular range from **C14** to **F14** to **F17** are the "mirror image" of the *lower* triangular range from **B15** to **B18** to **E18**. In other words, the correlation of Asset 2 with Asset 1 in C14 is equal to the correlation of Asset 1 with Asset 2 in B15. Enter **=B15** in cell **C14**, **=B16** in **D14**, **=B17** in **E14**, etc. Each cell of the *upper* triangular range from **C14** to **F14** to **F17** should be set equal to its mirror image cell in the *lower* triangular range from **B15** to **B18** to **E18**.

4.Transposed Standard Deviations. In addition to the standard deviation input range which runs vertically from top to bottom, it will be useful to have a range of standard deviations that runs horizontally from left-to-right. This can be done easily by using one of Excel's **Matrix** commands to transpose a range. Highlight the range **B22:F22**. Then, type **=TRANSPOSE (D6:D10)**, hold down the **Shift** and **Control** buttons simultaneously, and while continuing to hold them down, press **Enter**. The resulting formula should have braces around it **{=TRANSPOSE (D6:D10)}**.

5.Variances and Covariance's Table (Matrix). The Variances and Covariances Table (Matrix) in the range **B26:F30** has a simple structure. All of the elements on the diagonal represent the covariance of an asset return with itself, which equals the variance. For example, **B26** is the covariance of the Asset 1 return with the Asset 1 return, which equals the variance of asset 1. **C27** is the variance of Asset 2, and so on. The off-diagonal cells are covariances. For example, **C26** is the covariance of the Asset 1 return with the Asset 2 return and is calculated with the formula for the Covariance(Asset 1, Asset 2) = (Std Dev 1) * (Std Dev 2) * Correlation(Asset 1, Asset 2). Enter **=C$22*$D6*C14** in cell **C26**. Be very careful to enter the $ absolute references exactly right. Then copy **C26** to the range **B26:F30**.

FIGURE 2. Spreadsheet Details for Portfolio Optimization - Many Assets.

	A	B	C	D	E	F	G	H	I	J
36	Outputs									
37		A	125							
38		B	137.5							
39		C.	151.275		Efficient	Efficient				
40		Delta	3.1E+00		Frontier	Trade-off	Individual			
41		Gamma	0.13333		Curve	Line	Asset	Optimal Combination		
42				Standard	Expected	Expected	Expected	of Risky Assets		
43			Index	Deviation	Return	Return	Return	(Tangent Portfolio)		
44	Risky Asset 1			20.0%			8.0%	1	13.33%	
45	Risky Asset 2			20.0%			9.0%	2	16.67%	
46	Risky Asset 3			20.0%			10.0%	3	20.00%	
47	Risky Asset 4			20.0%			11.0%	4	23.33%	
48	Risky Asset 5			20.0%			12.0%	5	26.67%	
49	Trade-off Curve		0	25.00%	6.31%					
50	Trade-off Curve		1	22.84%	6.68%					
51	Trade-off Curve		2	20.71%	7.05%					
52	Trade-off Curve		3	18.63%	7.42%					
53	Trade-off Curve		4	16.62%	7.79%					
54	Trade-off Curve		5	14.71%	8.15%					
55	Trade-off Curve		6	12.93%	8.52%					
56	Trade-off Curve		7	11.36%	8.89%					
57	Trade-off Curve		8	10.09%	9.26%					
58	Trade-off Curve		9	9.24%	9.63%					
59	Trade-off Curve		10	8.94%	10.00%					
60	Trade-off Curve		11	9.24%	10.37%					
61	Trade-off Curve		12	10.09%	10.74%					
62	Trade-off Curve		13	11.36%	11.11%					
63	Trade-off Curve		14	12.93%	11.48%					
64	Trade-off Curve		15	14.71%	11.85%					
65	Trade-off Curve		16	16.62%	12.21%					
66	Trade-off Curve		17	18.63%	12.58%					
67	Trade-off Curve		18	20.71%	12.95%					
68	Trade-off Curve		19	22.84%	13.32%					
69	Trade-off Curve		20	25.00%	13.69%					
70	Optimal Comb.			9.2%		10.3%				
71	Eff Trade-off Line		0.0%	0.0%		4.0%				
72	Eff Trade-off Line		100.0%	9.2%		10.3%				
73	Eff Trade-off Line		200.0%	18.4%		16.7%				

6. Hyperbola Coefficients. In a Mean vs. Standard Deviation graph, the Efficient Frontier is a hyperbola. The exact location of the hyperbola is uniquely determined by three coefficients, unimaginatively called A, B, and C. The derivation of the formulas can be found in Merton (1972). [1] They are easy to implement using Excel's **matrix** functions. In each case, you type the formula and then, hold down the **Shift** and **Control** buttons simultaneously, and while continuing to hold them down, press **Enter**.

- For A: **=MMULT(MMULT(TRANSPOSE(F6:F10),MINVERSE(B26:F30)),F6:F10)** in cell **C37**.

- For B: **=MMULT(MMULT(TRANSPOSE(F6:F10),MINVERSE(B26:F30)),E6:E10)** in cell **C38**.

- For C: **=MMULT(MMULT(TRANSPOSE(E6:E10),MINVERSE(B26:F30)),E6:E10)** in cell **C39**.

7.Miscellaneous. It will simplify matters to create range names for various cells. Put the cursor in cell **C37**, click on **Insert Name Define**, enter the name "A" and click on **OK**. Repeat this procedure to give cell **C38** the name "B", give cell **C39** the name "C." (Excel does not accept plain "C"), give cell **C40** the name "**Delta**", give cell **C41** the name "**Gamma**", and give cell **E5** the name "R." (again, Excel does not accept plain "R"). Enter **=A*C.-(B^2)** in cell **C40** and enter **=1/(B-A*R.)** in cell **C41**. Some restrictions do apply on the range of permissible input values. The variable Delta must always be positive or else the calculations will blow-up or produce nonsense results. Simply avoid entering large negative correlations for multiple assets and this problem will be taken care of.

8.Individual Risky Assets. In order to add the individual risky assets to the graph, reference their individual standard deviations and expected returns. Enter **=D6** in cell **D44** and copy down to the range **D45:D48**. Enter **=C6** in cell **G44** and copy down to the range **G45:G48**.

9.Expected Return. Using the three Hyperbola coefficients, we can solve for the expected return on the upper and lower branches of the hyperbola which correspond to a standard deviation of **25%** and then fill in intermediate values in order to generate the Efficient Frontier graph.

- For the upper branch, enter **=(2*B-(4*B^2-4*A*(C.-(0.25^2)*Delta))^(0.5))/(2*A)-1** in cell **E49**.

- For the lower branch, enter **=(2*B+(4*B^2-4*A*(C.-(0.25^2)*Delta))^(0.5))/(2*A)-1** in cell **E69**.

- Fill out in index for expected return by entering **0** in cell **C49**, entering **1** in cell **C50**, selecting the range **C49:C50**, and dragging the fill handle (in the lower right corner) down the range **C51:C69**.

- Fill in the intermediate values by entering **=$E$49+($E$69-$E$49)*(C50/20)** in cell **E50** and copying the cell down the range **E51:E68**.

10.Standard Deviation. Again using the three Hyperbola coefficients, we can solve for the Efficient Frontier standard deviation which corresponds to any particular value of expected return. Enter **=((A*(1+E49)^2-(2*B*(1+E49))+C.)/(A*C.-(B^2)))^(1/2)** in cell **D49** and copy it down the range **D50:D69**.

11.Tangent Portfolio. The Optimal Combination of Risky Assets (or Tangent Portfolio) can be calculated using Excel's **matrix** functions. In each case, you type the formula and then, hold down the **Shift** and **Control** buttons simultaneously, and while continuing to hold them down, press **Enter**.

- For the portfolio weights: Select the range **I44:I48**, then type **=Gamma * MMULT (MINVERSE(B26:F30), (E6:E10-R.*F6:F10))**

- For expected returns: enter **=MMULT(TRANSPOSE(I44:I48),E6:E10)-1** in cell **F70**.

- For standard deviations: enter **=SQRT (MMULT (MMULT (TRANSPOSE (I44:I48), B26:F30), I44:I48))** in cell **D70**.

12.Efficient Trade-Off Line. The Efficient Trade-Off Line is a combination of the Riskless Asset and the Risky Asset Optimal Combination. It can be calculated as follows:

- Enter **0.0%** in cell **C71**, **100.0%** in cell **C72**, and **200.0%** in cell **C73**.

- As before, the standard deviation formula simplifies to $\sigma = w\sigma_T$. Enter **=C71*$D$70** in cell **D71** and copy the cell to the range **D72:D73**.

- The Expected Return formula is $E(r) = E(r_T)w + r_f(1-w)$. Enter **=$F$70*C71+$C$5*(1-C71)** in cell **F71** and copy to the range **F72:F73**.

13.Create And Locate The Graphs. Highlight the range **D44:G73** and then choose **Insert Chart** from the main menu. Select an **XY(Scatter)** chart type and make other selections to complete the Chart Wizard. Place the graph in the range **G3:K19**. Highlight the range **I44:I48** and then choose **Insert Chart** from the main menu. Select a **Column** chart type and make other selections to complete the Chart Wizard. Place the graph in the range **G21:K34**. Optionally, one can format the graph as discussed in the previous section.

The graphs show several interesting things. First, look at the Efficient Frontier Curve. At a standard deviation of 20% (same as all of the individual assets), it is possible to achieve a mean return of nearly 13% despite the fact that 12% is the highest mean return offered by any individual asset. How is this possible? The answer is that it is possible to sell (or short sell) low mean return assets and use the proceeds to invest in high mean return assets. Said differently, put a negative portfolio weight (short sell) in low mean assets and "more than 100%" in high mean assets.

Second, the bar chart shows that the optimal (tangent) portfolio represents a trade-off between exploiting higher means vs. lowering risk by diversifying (e.g., spreading the investment across assets). On the one hand it is desirable to put a larger portfolio weight in those assets with higher mean assets (#4 and #5 in this example). On the other hand, spreading assets more (getting closer to 20% per each of the five risky assets) would lower the overall risk of the portfolio. Hence, the optimal portfolio does not put 100% in the high mean assets, nor does it put 20% in each asset, but instead finds the best trade-off possible between theses two goals.

Third, you should be delighted to find any mispriced assets, because these are delightful investment opportunities for you. Indeed, many investors spend money to collect information (do security analysis) which identifies mispriced assets. The bar chart shows you how to optimally exploit any mispriced assets that you find. Below is a list of experiments that you might wish to perform. Notice as you perform these experiments that the optimal portfolio exploits mispriced assets to the *appropriate degree*, but still makes the fundamental trade-off between gaining higher means vs. lowering risk by diversifying.

- What happens when an individual asset is *underpriced* (high mean return)?

- What happens when an individual asset is *overpriced* (low mean return)?

- Is it possible for a very low mean return to optimally generate a negative weight (short sell)?

- What happens when an individual asset is *mispriced* due to a low standard deviation?

- What happens when an individual asset is *mispriced* due to a high standard deviation?

- What happens when the riskless rate is lowered?

- What happens when the riskless rate is raised?

- What happens when risky assets 1 and 2 have a 99% correlation?

Fourth, in general terms the optimal (tangent) portfolio is *not* the same as the market portfolio. Each individual investor should determine his or her *own tangent portfolio* based on his or her own beliefs about asset means, standard deviations, and correlations. If an individual investor believes that an particular asset is mispriced, then this belief should be optimally exploited. Only under the special conditions and the restrictive assumptions of CAPM theory would the tangent portfolio also be the market portfolio.

Here are some additional projects / enhancements you can do:

- Obtain historical data for different asset classes (and/or assets in different countries) and calculate the means, standard deviations, and correlations. Then, forecast future means, standard deviations, and correlations using the historical data as your starting point, but making appropriate adjustments. Input those means, standard deviations, and correlations into the spreadsheet model in order to determine the optimal portfolio. If you have monthly data, you can switch from annual returns to monthly returns by simply entering the appropriate monthly returns numbers and then rescaling the graph appropriately (see how to format the graph scale in the previous section).

- Create a *Dynamic Chart* by adding "spinners" (see other *Dynamic Charts* for examples of how to do this)

- Expand the number of risky assets to any number that you want. For example, expanding to six risky assets simply involves adding a sixth: (1) expected return in cell **C11**, (2) standard deviation in cell **D11**, (3) one plus expected return in cell **E11**, (4) **100%** in cell **F11**, (5) row of correlations in the range **B19:F19** and column in the range **G14:G19**, (6) row of variances / covariances in the range **B31:F31** and column in the range **G26:G31**. Finally, reenter all of the matrix functions changing their references to the expanded ranges. Specifically, reenter matrix functions for: transposed standard deviations, A, B, C, tangent portfolio weights, tangent portfolio expected return, and tangent portfolio standard deviation.

[1] See Robert C. Merton, "An Analytic Derivation of the Efficient Portfolio Frontier," *Journal of Financial and Quantitative Analysis*, September 1972, pp. 1851-72. His article uses slightly different notation.

PORTFOLIO OPTIMIZATION
Dynamic Chart

If you increased the expected return of a risky asset, what would happen to the efficient frontier curve or the efficient trade-off line (tangent line)? What would happen if you increased the standard deviation of a risky asset? What would happen if you increased the correlation between risky assets? You can answer these questions and more by creating an *Dynamic Chart* using "spinners." Spinners are up-arrow / down-arrow buttons that allow you to easily change the inputs to the model with the click of a mouse. Then the spreadsheet recalculates the model and instantly redraws the model outputs on the graph.

FIGURE 1. Spreadsheet for Portfolio Optimization - Dynamic Chart.

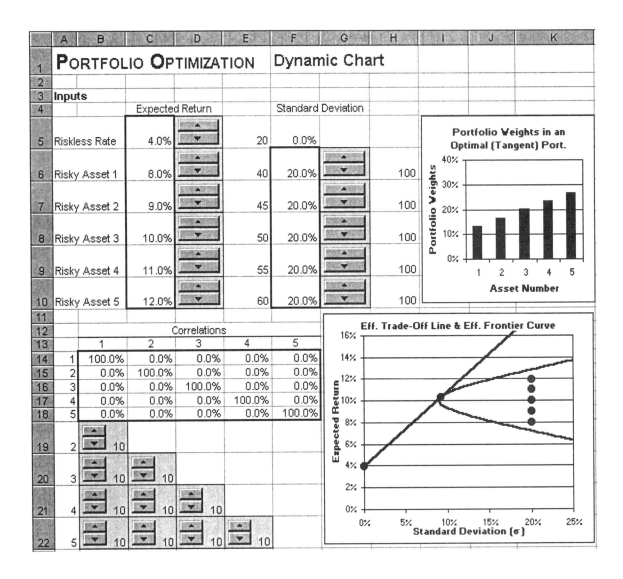

How To Build This Spreadsheet Model.

1.Start with the Many Assets Spreadsheet, Add Rows, and Rearrange A Bit. Open the spreadsheet that you created for Portfolio Optimization - Many Assets and immediately save the spreadsheet under a new name using the **File Save As** command. Move both of the graphs out of the way. Select each graph and drag them below row **22** and to the right of column **H**. Add four rows by selecting the range **A19:A22**, clicking on **Insert, Rows**. Select the range **E2:F10** and drag the range (hover the cursor over the lower highlighted line, click on the left mouse button, and hold it down while you move it) to cell **H26**. Select the range **D5:D10** and drag the range to cell **F5**.

2.Increase Row Height for the Spinners. Select the range **A5:A10**. Then click on **Format Row Height** from the main menu. Enter a height of **30** and click on **OK**. Select the range **A19:A22**. Then click on **Format Row Height** from the main menu. Enter a height of **30** and click on **OK**.

3.Display the Forms Toolbar. Select **View Toolbars Forms** from the main menu.

4.Create the Spinners. Look for the up-arrow / down-arrow button on the **Forms** toolbar (which will display the word "**Spinner**" if you hover the cursor over it) and click on it. Then draw the box for a spinner from the upper left corner of cell **D5** down to the lower right corner of the cell. Then a spinner appears in the cell **D5**. Right click on the spinner (press the right mouse button while the cursor is above the spinner) and a small menu pops up. Click on **Copy**. Then select the cell **D6** and click on **Paste**. This creates an identical spinner in the cell **D6**. Repeat the process four times more in cells **D7, D8, D9**, and **D10**. Repeat the process five times more in cells **G6, G7, G8, G9**, and **G10**. Click on the spinner button on the **Forms** toolbar and draw the box for a spinner covering the *left half* of cell **B19**. Click on **Copy**. Then select the cell **B20** and click on **Paste**. Repeat the process eight times more in cells **B21, B22, C20, C21, C22, D21, D22**, and **E22**.

5.Create The Cell Links. Right click on the first spinner in the cell **D5** and a small menu pops up. Click on **Format Control** and a dialog box pops up. Click on the **Control** tab, then enter the cell link **E5** in the **Cell link** edit box and click on **OK**. Repeat this procedure for the spinners in the range **D6:D10** and in the range **G6:G10** to link each one to the cell immediately to the right of each spinner. Right click on the spinner in the cell **B19** and a small menu pops up. Click on **Format Control** and a dialog box pops up. Click on the **Control** tab, then enter the *same cell* **B19** as the cell link in the **Cell link** edit box and click on **OK**. Repeat this *same cell* procedure for the spinners in the range **B20:B22** and in the triangle **C20** to **C22** to **E22** (linking each one to the same cell as the spinner). Test your spinners by clicking on the up-arrows and down-arrows of the spinners to see how they change the values in the linked cells.

6.Create Scaled Inputs. The values in the linked cells are always integers, but they can be scaled appropriately to the problem at hand. In cell **C5**, enter **=E5/500** and copy this cell to the range **C6:C10** and to the range **F6:F10**. In cell **B15**, enter **=B19/10-1** and copy the cell to the range **B20:B22** and to the triangle **C20** to **C22** to **E22**.

7.Relocate The Graphs. Move both of the graphs back into place. Move the Efficient Frontier graph into the range **G11:K22**. Move the Portfolio Weights graph into the range **I5:K10**.

Your *Dynamic Chart* allows you to change Portfolio Optimization inputs and instantly see the impact on a graphs of the efficient frontier and portfolio weights. This allows you to perform instant experiments on the efficient frontier and portfolio weights. The portfolio weights of the optimal (tangent) portfolio are a trade-off between putting more in assets with higher expected returns vs. spreading investment out evenly to lower portfolio risk by diversification. You can see how this trade-off works by doing some of the experiments listed below:

- What happens to the optimal portfolio weight of an individual asset that is *underpriced* (e.g., the expected return is raised)?

- What happens to the optimal portfolio weight of an individual asset that is *overpriced* (e.g., the expected return is lowered)?

- What happens to the optimal portfolio weight of an individual asset that is *mispriced* due to the standard deviation of the asset being raised?

- What happens to the optimal portfolio weight of an individual asset that is *mispriced* due to the standard deviation of the asset being lowered?

- What happens to the optimal portfolio weights of two risky assets when the correlation between them is raised?

- What happens to the optimal portfolio weights of two risky assets when the correlation between them is lowered?

- What happens to the efficient trade-off (tangent) line when the riskfree rate is raised?

- What happens to the efficient trade-off (tangent) line when the riskfree rate is lowered?

PORTFOLIO OPTIMIZATION
Full-Scale Real Data

The mean-variance optimization technique is a very general technique that can be used to find the optimal portfolio investment for any number of risky assets and any type of risky asset: stocks, corporate bonds, international bonds, real estate, commodities, etc.

Problem Using Real Data. The key inputs required are the means, standard deviations, and correlations of the risky assets. These inputs must be estimated from historical data. Typically, one would use five years of monthly data. Using only one or two years worth of data provide enough observations to have reliable estimates. Another difficulty is that means, standard deviations, and correlations evolve over time. So using ten years of data would produce unstable estimates because you are averaging across different "regimes". Five years of data is a good compromise. What are the portfolio weights of the optimal (tangent) portfolio?

FIGURE 1. Spreadsheet for Portfolio Optimization - Estimating Means, Std Devs, and Corrs.

	A	B	C	D	E	V	W	X	Y	Z	AA	AB
1	**PORTFOLIO OPTIMIZATION**					**Estimating Means, Std Devs, and Corrs**						
2												
3	Date	CS	CBT	COG	CBE.TO		CS	CBT	COG	CBE.TO	CACI	CSG
4	Dec-99	26.0000	20.3750	16.0625	12.0000		14.29%	6.89%	4.90%	7.14%	2.84%	-1.28%
5	Nov-99	22.7500	19.0625	15.3125	11.2000		36.33%	2.94%	-4.81%	-8.57%	2.62%	-6.22%
6	Oct-99	16.6875	18.5175	16.0859	12.2500		6.37%	-21.58%	-6.52%	-17.51%	0.59%	-5.64%
7	Sep-99	15.6875	23.6130	17.2082	14.8500		-6.69%	2.98%	-9.51%	-9.45%	-5.28%	9.11%
8	Aug-99	16.8125	22.9294	19.0163	16.4000		39.38%	-3.46%	5.77%	1.86%	2.86%	-0.43%
9	Jul-99	12.0625	23.7513	17.9787	16.1000		-7.21%	-0.77%	-3.02%	15.00%	-2.78%	-3.52%
10	Jun-99	13.0000	23.9368	18.5386	14.0000		-12.61%	2.38%	4.20%	16.67%	22.45%	-3.95%
11	May-99	14.8750	23.3802	17.7920	12.0000		57.62%	-12.12%	2.38%	-14.89%	1.38%	2.66%
12	Apr-99	9.4375	26.6044	17.3790	14.1000		15.27%	27.06%	21.21%	8.46%	7.01%	-7.00%
13	Mar-99	8.1875	20.9386	14.3376	13.0000		0.77%	-15.63%	32.00%	30.00%	2.65%	-5.51%
14	Feb-99	8.1250	24.8184	10.8619	10.0000		-22.16%	0.69%	-16.42%	-11.50%	-10.51%	-2.35%
15	Jan-99	10.4375	24.6479	12.9952	11.3000		24.63%	-10.07%	-12.50%	0.00%	9.26%	-7.60%
54	Oct-95	39.3125	22.2892	12.8599	12.7500		19.35%	-10.59%	-1.84%	-1.92%	-9.62%	8.54%
55	Sep-95	32.9375	24.9287	13.1003	13.0000		24.59%	10.39%	-6.03%	-7.14%	5.05%	-0.33%
56	Aug-95	26.4375	22.5825	13.9416	14.0000		0.00%	-14.33%	3.88%	1.82%	7.61%	-1.58%
57	Jul-95	26.4375	26.3602	13.4209	13.7500		-0.70%	6.87%	1.82%	-8.33%	-6.12%	6.30%
58	Jun-95	26.6250	24.6652	13.1813	15.0000		-0.47%	25.22%	-12.70%	5.26%	19.51%	-0.59%
59	May-95	26.7500	19.6971	15.0985	14.2500		12.63%	7.69%	1.88%	0.00%	2.50%	5.00%
60	Apr-95	23.7500	18.2907	14.8202	14.2500		5.85%	6.44%	-0.80%	4.55%	8.11%	0.00%
61	Mar-95	22.4375	17.1839	14.9397	13.6300		13.25%	8.46%	13.64%	13.58%	-2.63%	6.48%
62	Feb-95	19.8125	15.8442	13.1470	12.0000		4.28%	11.47%	10.32%	-2.04%	-4.40%	5.41%
63	Jan-95	19.0000	14.2133	11.9167	12.2500							
64												
65	Ave Ret						2.50%	1.16%	1.05%	0.38%	1.92%	1.46%
66	Std Dev						20.23%	10.62%	10.54%	9.29%	10.32%	6.03%
67												
68	Corr						*Column 1*	*Column 2*	*Column 3*	*Column 4*	*Column 5*	*Column 6*
69						Column 1	1					
70						Column 2	0.1558	1				
71						Column 3	0.3928	0.20506	1			
72						Column 4	0.0327	0.15092	0.44365	1		
73						Column 5	0.2916	0.1421	0.23574	0.21843	1	
74						Column 6	-0.1325	0.13233	0.07206	-0.1148	-0.1505	1

Solution Strategy. Collect historical stock prices for 20 companies from Yahoo Finance! and calculate the sample means, standard deviations, and correlations. Expand the Portfolio Optimization - Many Assets model from 5 risky assets to 20 risky assets. Then copy the estimated values of means, standard deviations, and correlations into the input area.

How To Build This Spreadsheet Model.

1.Collect Historical Stock Price Data For 20 Firms. Go to Yahoo Finance! (quote.yahoo.com), click on **symbol lookup**, click on **alphabetical listing**, and click on a letter (such as **C**) to get a list of company names and their corresponding ticker symbols. For example, the stock symbol for Cabletron Systems Inc is **CS**. Click back to the home page of Yahoo Finance! and under **Research** click on **Historical Quotes**. Enter a **Start Date** and **End Date** to give you a five year span of time, click on the **Monthly** radio button, and enter a ticker symbol, such as **CS**, in the **Ticker Symbol** box, click on **Get Historical Data**. It displays five years of monthly data on the firm (if available). Importantly, the monthly data includes the "Adjusted Close" price, which is adjusted for stock splits and dividends. Verify that the data goes back for the full five years, then click on **Download Spreadsheet Format**, enter a name for the comma-delimited csv file, such as **cs.csv**, and click on **Save**. By default, the Adjusted Close price is what gets downloaded. Repeat this process for 20 Firms. Launch Excel and open the each csv file. Copy the column of "Close" prices (which is actually the "Adjusted Close") from each csv file to a common Excel file and label each column with the ticker symbol. In Figure 1, columns B through U are the monthly (adjusted) close price for 20 firms.

2.Monthly Returns. The formula for a Monthly Return = (Price Now - Price Last Month) / (Price Last Month). Enter **=(B4-B5)/B5** in cell **W4** and copy the cell to the range **W4:AP62**.

3.Expected Returns and Standard Deviations. Estimate the expected returns and standard deviations next period by calculating the sample average returns and sample standard deviation in the historical data. Enter **=AVERAGE(W4:W62)** in cell **W65** and copy the cell to the range **X65:AP65**. Enter **=STDEV(W4:W62)** in cell **W66** and copy the cell to the range **X66:AP66**.

4.Correlations. Estimate the correlations next period by calculating the sample correlations in the historical data. Click on **Tools Data Analysis Correlations OK** (if **Data Analysis** does not appear on the **Tools** menu, then Click on **Tools, Add-Ins**, check the **Analysis ToolPak** checkbox, and click on OK). In the **Correlation** dialog box, enter **W4:AP62** in the **Input Range** box, click on the **Output Range** radio button, enter **V68** in the **Output Range box**, and click on **OK**. A correlations table (matrix) is generated from the historical data with only the lower-left triangle filled in.

FIGURE 2. Spreadsheet for Portfolio Optimization - Estimating Means, Std Devs, and Corrs (Continued).

		V	W	X	Y	Z	AA	AB	AC	AD
90			Column 1	Column 2	Column 3	Column 4	Column 5	Column 6	Column 7	Column 8
91	Column 1	1.0000	0.1558	0.3928	0.0327	0.2916	-0.1325	0.3404	0.4051
92	Column 2	0.0000	1.0000	0.2051	0.1509	0.1421	0.1323	-0.0397	0.0675
93	Column 3	0.0000	0.0000	1.0000	0.4436	0.2357	0.0721	0.3063	0.1659
94	Column 4	0.0000	0.0000	0.0000	1.0000	0.2184	-0.1148	-0.0488	0.0603
95	Column 5	0.0000	0.0000	0.0000	0.0000	1.0000	-0.1505	0.3251	0.1444
96	Column 6	0.0000	0.0000	0.0000	0.0000	0.0000	1.0000	-0.2058	0.0839
97	Column 7	0.0000	0.0000	0.0000	0.0000	0.0000	0.0000	1.0000	0.3067
98	Column 8	0.0000	0.0000	0.0000	0.0000	0.0000	0.0000	0.0000	1.0000
99	Column 9	0.0000	0.0000	0.0000	0.0000	0.0000	0.0000	0.0000	0.0000
100	Column 10	0.0000	0.0000	0.0000	0.0000	0.0000	0.0000	0.0000	0.0000
101	Column 11	0.0000	0.0000	0.0000	0.0000	0.0000	0.0000	0.0000	0.0000
102	Column 12	0.0000	0.0000	0.0000	0.0000	0.0000	0.0000	0.0000	0.0000
103	Column 13	0.0000	0.0000	0.0000	0.0000	0.0000	0.0000	0.0000	0.0000
104	Column 14	0.0000	0.0000	0.0000	0.0000	0.0000	0.0000	0.0000	0.0000
105	Column 15	0.0000	0.0000	0.0000	0.0000	0.0000	0.0000	0.0000	0.0000
106	Column 16	0.0000	0.0000	0.0000	0.0000	0.0000	0.0000	0.0000	0.0000
107	Column 17	0.0000	0.0000	0.0000	0.0000	0.0000	0.0000	0.0000	0.0000
108	Column 18	0.0000	0.0000	0.0000	0.0000	0.0000	0.0000	0.0000	0.0000
109	Column 19	0.0000	0.0000	0.0000	0.0000	0.0000	0.0000	0.0000	0.0000
110	Column 20	0.0000	0.0000	0.0000	0.0000	0.0000	0.0000	0.0000	0.0000
111										
112			Column 1	Column 2	Column 3	Column 4	Column 5	Column 6	Column 7	Column 8
113	Column 1	1.0000	0.1558	0.3928	0.0327	0.2916	-0.1325	0.3404	0.4051
114	Column 2	0.1558	1.0000	0.2051	0.1509	0.1421	0.1323	-0.0397	0.0675
115	Column 3	0.3928	0.2051	1.0000	0.4436	0.2357	0.0721	0.3063	0.1659
116	Column 4	0.0327	0.1509	0.4436	1.0000	0.2184	-0.1148	-0.0488	0.0603
117	Column 5	0.2916	0.1421	0.2357	0.2184	1.0000	-0.1505	0.3251	0.1444
118	Column 6	-0.1325	0.1323	0.0721	-0.1148	-0.1505	1.0000	-0.2058	0.0839
119	Column 7	0.3404	-0.0397	0.3063	-0.0488	0.3251	-0.2058	1.0000	0.3067
120	Column 8	0.4051	0.0675	0.1659	0.0603	0.1444	0.0839	0.3067	1.0000
121	Column 9	-0.0592	0.2853	0.2036	0.2346	0.2135	0.3283	-0.0183	0.1850
122	Column 10	0.1560	0.3107	0.1812	0.1932	0.1566	-0.1178	0.1487	0.0273
123	Column 11	0.2163	0.2176	-0.0133	-0.0890	0.3105	-0.0201	0.0592	0.3105
124	Column 12	0.2161	0.1758	0.1951	0.0744	0.1072	0.1050	0.0508	-0.2370
125	Column 13	0.0997	0.0579	0.0482	-0.0156	-0.0171	-0.0516	0.3544	0.0573
126	Column 14	0.3127	0.4293	0.3888	0.1432	0.2998	-0.0092	0.3720	0.1725
127	Column 15	0.3863	0.3064	0.3232	0.2963	0.2141	-0.2841	0.2278	0.1833
128	Column 16	-0.0194	0.0093	0.1669	0.1619	0.0460	0.1707	-0.0953	0.1779
129	Column 17	0.1142	0.0163	0.1635	-0.0801	0.2444	0.0960	0.0370	0.0558
130	Column 18	0.3645	0.4268	0.1902	0.0152	0.2579	-0.1394	0.0645	0.0939
131	Column 19	0.3852	0.2741	0.5501	0.2997	0.2077	-0.0285	0.4071	0.3555
132	Column 20	-0.0464	0.1749	0.1631	-0.0561	0.0234	0.2142	0.0159	0.0505

5.Transposed Correlations. The simplest way to get a complete Correlations Matrix is to transpose the lower-left triangle of correlations to the upper-right triangle of correlations. Highlight the range **W91:AP110** and enter **=TRANSPOSE(W69:AP88)**. Then, hold down the **Shift** and **Control** buttons simultaneously, and while continuing to hold them down, press **Enter**. The resulting formula should have braces around it **{=TRANSPOSE(W69:AP88)}**.

6.Complete Correlations. The complete correlations table (matrix) can be constructed simply by adding the lower-left triangle to the upper right triangle and eliminating the double-counting on the diagonal strip. Enter **=IF(W69+W91=2,1,W69+W91)** in cell **W113** and copy the cell to the range **W113:AP132**.

FIGURE 3. Spreadsheet for Portfolio Optimization - Full-Scale Real Data.

	A	B	C	D	E	F	G H I J K
1	**PORTFOLIO OPTIMIZATION**					**Full-Scale Real Data**	
2					One plus		
3	**Inputs**		Expected	Standard	Exp Ret		
4			Return	Deviation	[1 + E(r)]	Ones	
5	Riskless Rate (r)		0.3%	0.0%	100.3%		
6	Risky Asset 1		2.5%	20.2%	102.5%	100.0%	
7	Risky Asset 2		1.2%	10.6%	101.2%	100.0%	
8	Risky Asset 3		1.0%	10.5%	101.0%	100.0%	
9	Risky Asset 4		0.4%	9.3%	100.4%	100.0%	
10	Risky Asset 5		1.9%	10.3%	101.9%	100.0%	
11	Risky Asset 6		1.5%	6.0%	101.5%	100.0%	
12	Risky Asset 7		5.0%	18.0%	105.0%	100.0%	
13	Risky Asset 8		4.0%	15.3%	104.0%	100.0%	
14	Risky Asset 9		-0.3%	11.2%	99.7%	100.0%	
15	Risky Asset 10		1.0%	6.6%	101.0%	100.0%	
16	Risky Asset 11		0.9%	17.6%	100.9%	100.0%	
17	Risky Asset 12		-0.4%	11.4%	99.6%	100.0%	
18	Risky Asset 13		-6.7%	20.6%	93.3%	100.0%	
19	Risky Asset 14		-0.2%	9.7%	99.8%	100.0%	
20	Risky Asset 15		7.3%	27.3%	107.3%	100.0%	
21	Risky Asset 16		-0.2%	10.0%	99.8%	100.0%	
22	Risky Asset 17		1.8%	7.3%	101.8%	100.0%	
23	Risky Asset 18		1.3%	14.1%	101.3%	100.0%	
24	Risky Asset 19		1.6%	14.3%	101.6%	100.0%	
25	Risky Asset 20		1.7%	17.1%	101.7%	100.0%	
26							

Eff. Trade-Off Line & Eff. Frontier Curve (Expected Return vs Standard Deviation (σ))

	A	B	C	D	E	F	G	H	I	J	K
27		Correlations									
28			1	2	3	4	5	6	7	8	9	10
29		1	100.0%	15.6%	39.3%	3.3%	29.2%	-13.2%	34.0%	40.5%	-5.9%	15.6%
30		2	15.6%	100.0%	20.5%	15.1%	14.2%	13.2%	-4.0%	6.7%	28.5%	31.1%
31		3	39.3%	20.5%	100.0%	44.4%	23.6%	7.2%	30.6%	16.6%	20.4%	18.1%
32		4	3.3%	15.1%	44.4%	100.0%	21.8%	-11.5%	-4.9%	6.0%	23.5%	19.3%
33		5	29.2%	14.2%	23.6%	21.8%	100.0%	-15.0%	32.5%	14.4%	21.4%	15.7%
34		6	-13.2%	13.2%	7.2%	-11.5%	-15.0%	100.0%	-20.6%	8.4%	32.8%	-11.8%
35		7	34.0%	-4.0%	30.6%	-4.9%	32.5%	-20.6%	100.0%	30.7%	-1.8%	14.9%
36		8	40.5%	6.7%	16.6%	6.0%	14.4%	8.4%	30.7%	100.0%	18.5%	2.7%
37		9	-5.9%	28.5%	20.4%	23.5%	21.4%	32.8%	-1.8%	18.5%	100.0%	9.4%
38		10	15.6%	31.1%	18.1%	19.3%	15.7%	-11.8%	14.9%	2.7%	9.4%	100.0%
39		11	21.6%	21.8%	-1.3%	-8.9%	31.1%	-2.0%	5.9%	31.0%	22.0%	7.0%
40		12	21.6%	17.6%	19.5%	7.4%	10.7%	10.5%	5.1%	-23.7%	6.5%	11.0%
41		13	10.0%	5.8%	4.8%	-1.6%	-1.7%	-5.2%	35.4%	5.7%	9.4%	13.0%
42		14	31.3%	42.9%	38.9%	14.3%	30.0%	-0.9%	37.2%	17.3%	10.9%	20.0%
43		15	38.6%	30.6%	32.3%	29.6%	21.4%	-28.4%	22.8%	18.3%	-0.4%	21.7%
44		16	-1.9%	0.9%	16.7%	16.2%	4.6%	17.1%	-9.5%	17.8%	16.1%	16.0%
45		17	11.4%	1.6%	16.3%	-8.0%	24.4%	9.6%	3.7%	5.6%	6.2%	-4.0%
46		18	36.5%	42.7%	19.0%	1.5%	25.8%	-13.9%	6.5%	9.4%	0.8%	27.1%
47		19	38.5%	27.4%	55.0%	30.0%	20.8%	-2.8%	40.7%	35.6%	21.3%	13.1%
48		20	-4.6%	17.5%	16.3%	-5.6%	2.3%	21.4%	1.6%	5.0%	20.1%	11.9%

7. Open the Many Assets Spreadsheet, Add Rows, and Update the Riskless Rate. Open the spreadsheet that you created for Portfolio Optimization - Many Assets and immediately save the spreadsheet under a new name using the **File Save As** command. Move the Efficient Frontier graph out of the way by clicking on it and dragging it below row **32** and to the right of column **V**. Delete the Portfolio Weights graph by clicking on it and pressing the **Delete** button. Add fifteen rows to the Outputs area by selecting the range **A49:A63** and clicking on **Insert Rows**. Add fifteen rows for the Correlations by selecting the range **A19:A33** and clicking on **Insert Rows**. Add fifteen rows for the Expected Returns and Standard Deviations by selecting the range **A11:A25** and clicking on **Insert Rows**. Lookup the yield to maturity of a Treasury Bill with one month to maturity in the financial press. To convert this annualized yield to maturity to a monthly rate, divide by 12. (The *Wall Street Journal* and most financial press use the annual percentage rate convention.) Enter this value in cell **C5**.

8.Copy the Means, Standard Deviations, and Correlations Over. Copy the estimated values of the Means, Standard Deviations, and Correlations from the estimation spreadsheet to the Full-Scale Real Data spreadsheet. Select the range **W65:AP66** of the **Estimating Means**, **Std Devs**, **and Corrs** spreadsheet, click on **Edit Copy**, select the cell **C6**, of the **Full-Scale Real Data** spreadsheet, click on **Edit Paste Special**, in the **Paste** section of the dialog box click on **Values** and near the bottom click on **Transpose** and **OK**. Select the range **W113:AP132** of the **Estimating Means**, **Std Devs**, **and Corrs** spreadsheet, click on **Edit Copy**, select the cell **B29**, of the **Full-Scale Real Data** spreadsheet, click on **Edit Paste Special**, in the **Paste** section of the dialog box click on **Values** and **OK**.

9.One plus the Expected Return and 100%. Copy the formulas for One plus the Expected Return and 100% down the columns. Select the range **E6:F6** and copy it to the range **E7:F25**.

FIGURE 4. Spreadsheet Details for Portfolio Optimization - Full-Scale Real Data.

	A	B	C	D	E	F	G	H	I	J	K
50		Standard Deviations									
51		1	2	3	4	5	6	7	8	9	10
52		20.2%	10.6%	10.5%	9.3%	10.3%	6.0%	18.0%	15.3%	11.2%	6.6%
53											
54		Variances and Covariances									
55		1	2	3	4	5	6	7	8	9	10
56	1	4.09%	0.33%	0.84%	0.06%	0.61%	-0.16%	1.24%	1.26%	-0.13%	0.21%
57	2	0.33%	1.13%	0.23%	0.15%	0.16%	0.08%	-0.08%	0.11%	0.34%	0.22%
58	3	0.84%	0.23%	1.11%	0.43%	0.26%	0.05%	0.58%	0.27%	0.24%	0.13%
59	4	0.06%	0.15%	0.43%	0.86%	0.21%	-0.06%	-0.08%	0.09%	0.24%	0.12%
60	5	0.61%	0.16%	0.26%	0.21%	1.07%	-0.09%	0.60%	0.23%	0.25%	0.11%
61	6	-0.16%	0.08%	0.05%	-0.06%	-0.09%	0.36%	-0.22%	0.08%	0.22%	-0.05%
62	7	1.24%	-0.08%	0.58%	-0.08%	0.60%	-0.22%	3.23%	0.84%	-0.04%	0.18%
63	8	1.26%	0.11%	0.27%	0.09%	0.23%	0.08%	0.84%	2.35%	0.32%	0.03%
64	9	-0.13%	0.34%	0.24%	0.24%	0.25%	0.22%	-0.04%	0.32%	1.26%	0.07%
65	10	0.21%	0.22%	0.13%	0.12%	0.11%	-0.05%	0.18%	0.03%	0.07%	0.43%
66	11	0.77%	0.41%	-0.02%	-0.15%	0.57%	-0.02%	0.19%	0.84%	0.44%	0.08%
67	12	0.50%	0.21%	0.23%	0.08%	0.13%	0.07%	0.10%	-0.41%	0.08%	0.08%
68	13	0.42%	0.13%	0.10%	-0.03%	-0.04%	-0.06%	1.31%	0.18%	0.22%	0.18%
69	14	0.61%	0.44%	0.40%	0.13%	0.30%	-0.01%	0.65%	0.26%	0.12%	0.13%
70	15	2.14%	0.89%	0.93%	0.75%	0.60%	-0.47%	1.12%	0.77%	-0.01%	0.39%
71	16	-0.04%	0.01%	0.18%	0.15%	0.05%	0.10%	-0.17%	0.27%	0.18%	0.11%
72	17	0.17%	0.01%	0.13%	-0.05%	0.18%	0.04%	0.05%	0.06%	0.05%	-0.02%
73	18	1.04%	0.64%	0.28%	0.02%	0.38%	-0.12%	0.16%	0.20%	0.01%	0.25%
74	19	1.11%	0.42%	0.83%	0.40%	0.31%	-0.02%	1.05%	0.78%	0.34%	0.12%
75	20	-0.16%	0.32%	0.29%	-0.09%	0.04%	0.22%	0.05%	0.13%	0.38%	0.13%

10.Transposed Standard Deviations. Extend the range of standard deviations that runs horizontally from left-to-right. Highlight the range **B52:U52**. Press the **F2** key, edit the formula so that it reads **=TRANSPOSE(D6:D25)**, hold down the **Shift** and **Control** buttons simultaneously, and while continuing to hold them down, press **Enter**. The resulting formula should have braces around it **{=TRANSPOSE(D6:D25)}**.

11.Variances and Covariance's Table (Matrix). Extend the Variances and Covariances Table (Matrix). Select the cell **B56** and copy the cell to the range **B56:U75**.

FIGURE 5. Spreadsheet Details for Portfolio Optimization - Full-Scale Real Data.

	A	B	C	D	E	F	G	H	I	J
81	Outputs									
82		A	1076.96							
83		B	1090.49							
84		C.	1104.8		Efficient	Efficient				
85		Delta	6.4E+02		Frontier	Trade-off	Individual			
86		Gamma	0.09703		Curve	Line	Asset		Optimal Combination	
87				Standard	Expected	Expected	Expected		of Risky Assets	
88			Index	Deviation	Return	Return	Return		(Tangent Portfolio)	
89	Risky Asset 1			20.2%			2.5%	1	-1.0%	
90	Risky Asset 2			10.6%			1.2%	2	10.4%	
91	Risky Asset 3			10.5%			1.0%	3	-35.0%	
92	Risky Asset 4			9.3%			0.4%	4	10.3%	
93	Risky Asset 5			10.3%			1.9%	5	1.0%	
94	Risky Asset 6			6.0%			1.5%	6	80.9%	
95	Risky Asset 7			18.0%			5.0%	7	35.4%	
96	Risky Asset 8			15.3%			4.0%	8	-6.1%	
97	Risky Asset 9			11.2%			-0.3%	9	-15.7%	
98	Risky Asset 10			6.6%			1.0%	10	13.9%	
99	Risky Asset 11			17.6%			0.9%	11	-1.4%	
100	Risky Asset 12			11.4%			-0.4%	12	-15.4%	
101	Risky Asset 13			20.6%			-6.7%	13	-28.3%	
102	Risky Asset 14			9.7%			-0.2%	14	-44.5%	
103	Risky Asset 15			27.3%			7.3%	15	18.0%	
104	Risky Asset 16			10.0%			-0.2%	16	15.5%	
105	Risky Asset 17			7.3%			1.8%	17	32.1%	
106	Risky Asset 18			14.1%			1.3%	18	3.5%	
107	Risky Asset 19			14.3%			1.6%	19	21.1%	
108	Risky Asset 20			17.1%			1.7%	20	5.0%	
109	Trade-off Curve	0	25.00%	-17.91%						
110	Trade-off Curve	1	22.54%	-15.99%						
111	Trade-off Curve	2	20.08%	-14.07%						
112	Trade-off Curve	3	17.63%	-12.16%						
113	Trade-off Curve	4	15.20%	-10.24%						
114	Trade-off Curve	5	12.78%	-8.32%						
115	Trade-off Curve	6	10.38%	-6.41%						
116	Trade-off Curve	7	8.04%	-4.49%						
117	Trade-off Curve	8	5.82%	-2.58%						
118	Trade-off Curve	9	3.93%	-0.66%						
119	Trade-off Curve	10	3.05%	1.26%						
120	Trade-off Curve	11	3.93%	3.17%						
121	Trade-off Curve	12	5.82%	5.09%						
122	Trade-off Curve	13	8.04%	7.01%						
123	Trade-off Curve	14	10.38%	8.92%						
124	Trade-off Curve	15	12.78%	10.84%						
125	Trade-off Curve	16	15.20%	12.75%						
126	Trade-off Curve	17	17.63%	14.67%						
127	Trade-off Curve	18	20.08%	16.59%						
128	Trade-off Curve	19	22.54%	18.50%						
129	Trade-off Curve	20	25.00%	20.42%						

12.Hyperbola Coefficients. Extend the ranges in the three hyperbola coefficients, A, B, and C. They are implemented using Excel's **matrix** functions. In each case, you type the formula and then, hold down the **Shift** and **Control** buttons simultaneously, and while continuing to hold them down, press **Enter**.

- For A: **=MMULT(MMULT(TRANSPOSE(F6:F25),MINVERSE(B56:U75)), F6:F25)** in cell **C82**.

- For B: **=MMULT(MMULT(TRANSPOSE(F6:F25),MINVERSE(B56:U75)), E6:E25)** in cell **C83**.

- For C: **=MMULT(MMULT(TRANSPOSE(E6:E25),MINVERSE(B56:U75)), E6:E25)** in cell **C84**.

13.Individual Risky Assets. Extend the individual risky assets in the Outputs section. Select the range **D93:G93** and copy it to the range **D94:D108**.

FIGURE 6. Spreadsheet Details for Portfolio Optimization - Full-Scale Real Data.

	A B	C	D	E	F
109	Trade-off Curve	0	25.00%	-17.91%	
110	Trade-off Curve	1	22.54%	-15.99%	
111	Trade-off Curve	2	20.08%	-14.07%	
112	Trade-off Curve	3	17.63%	-12.16%	
113	Trade-off Curve	4	15.20%	-10.24%	
114	Trade-off Curve	5	12.78%	-8.32%	
115	Trade-off Curve	6	10.38%	-6.41%	
116	Trade-off Curve	7	8.04%	-4.49%	
117	Trade-off Curve	8	5.82%	-2.58%	
118	Trade-off Curve	9	3.93%	-0.66%	
119	Trade-off Curve	10	3.05%	1.26%	
120	Trade-off Curve	11	3.93%	3.17%	
121	Trade-off Curve	12	5.82%	5.09%	
122	Trade-off Curve	13	8.04%	7.01%	
123	Trade-off Curve	14	10.38%	8.92%	
124	Trade-off Curve	15	12.78%	10.84%	
125	Trade-off Curve	16	15.20%	12.75%	
126	Trade-off Curve	17	17.63%	14.67%	
127	Trade-off Curve	18	20.08%	16.59%	
128	Trade-off Curve	19	22.54%	18.50%	
129	Trade-off Curve	20	25.00%	20.42%	
130	Optimal Comb.		8.1%		7.0%
131	Eff Trade-off Line	0.0%	0.0%		0.3%
132	Eff Trade-off Line	100.0%	8.1%		7.0%
133	Eff Trade-off Line	500.0%	40.4%		34.0%

14.Tangent Portfolio. The Optimal Combination of Risky Assets (or Tangent Portfolio) can be calculated using Excel's **matrix** functions. In each case, you type the formula and then, hold down the **Shift** and **Control** buttons simultaneously, and while continuing to hold them down, press **Enter**.

- For the portfolio weights: Select the range **I89:I108**, then type **=Gamma*MMULT (MINVERSE(B56:U75), (E6:E25-R.*F6:F25))**

- For expected returns: enter **=MMULT(TRANSPOSE(I89:I108), E6:E25)-1** in cell **F130**.

- For standard deviations: enter **=SQRT(MMULT(MMULT(TRANSPOSE(I89:I108), B56:U75), I89:I108))** in cell **D130**.

15.Efficient Trade-Off Line. Extend the Efficient Trade-Off Line. Enter **500.0%** in cell **C133**.

16. Relocate The Graphs. Move the graph back into place. Move the Efficient Frontier graph into the range **G6:K22**.

The portfolio weights of the optimal (tangent) portfolio are listed in the range **I89:I108** (see Figure 5). You will notice large positive weights on those assets with high expected returns ("past winners") and/or low standard deviation. Similarly, there are large negative weights (meaning short selling) on those assets with low expected returns ("past losers") and/or high standard deviation. One problem with directly using the estimates from historical data is that you get rather extreme portfolio weights (for example, 80.9% in asset 6 and -44.5% in asset 14). Essentially, this assumes that past winners will win just as big in future and past losers will lose just as big in the future. A standard "Bayesian" technique for dealing with this estimation problem is to lower the future expected returns on past winners and raise the future expected returns on past losers. Shifting all of the estimates in the direction of the middle will yield much more reasonable portfolio weights for the optimal (tangent) portfolio.

PORTFOLIO OPTIMIZATION
Problems

Problems To Build And Use The Spreadsheet Models

1. The riskless rate is 5.1%. Risky Asset 1 has a mean return of 11.3% and a standard deviation of 23.2%. Risky Asset 2 has a mean return of 6.9% and a standard deviation of 18.7%. The correlation between Risky Asset 1 and 2 is 24.5%. Build the **Portfolio Optimization - Two Asset** model, including a graph the Efficient Trade-Off Line and the Risky Asset Trade-Off Curve.

2. The riskless rate is 4.7%. There are five risky assets. Their expected returns are 11.3%, 7.8%, 9.2%, 13.6%, and 10.5%. Their standard deviations are 16.6%, 24.3%, 19.7%, 22.9%, and 18.3%. All of the correlations are 0.0%, except the correlation between risky assets 2 and 5 which is 18.2%. Build the **Portfolio Optimization - Many Asset** model, including a graph the Efficient Trade-Off Line and the Risky Asset Trade-Off Curve and a bar chart of the portfolio weights of the optimal (tangent) portfolio.

3. Build the **Portfolio Optimization - Dynamic Chart** model and use it to perform instant experiments on the efficient frontier and portfolio weights. The portfolio weights of the optimal (tangent) portfolio are a trade-off between putting more in assets with higher expected returns vs. spreading investment out evenly to lower portfolio risk by diversification. You can see how this trade-off works by doing some of the experiments listed below:

(a.) What happens to the optimal portfolio weight of an individual asset that is underpriced (e.g. the expected return is raised)?

(b.) What happens to the optimal portfolio weight of an individual asset that is overpriced (e.g. the expected return is lowered)?

(c.) What happens to the optimal portfolio weight of an individual asset that is mispriced due to the standard deviation of the asset being raised?

(d.) What happens to the optimal portfolio weight of an individual asset that is mispriced due to the standard deviation of the asset being lowered?

(e.) What happens to the optimal portfolio weights of two risky assets when the correlation between them is raised?

(f.) What happens to the optimal portfolio weights of two risky assets when the correlation between them is lowered?

(g.) What happens to the efficient trade-off (tangent) line when the riskfree rate is raised?

(h.) What happens to the efficient trade-off (tangent) line when the riskfree rate is lowered?

4. Collect historical stock prices for 20 companies of your own choosing from Yahoo Finance! and calculate the sample means, standard deviations, and correlations. Build the **Portfolio Optimization - Full-Scale Real Data** model and use it to determine the portfolio weights of the optimal (tangent) portfolio.

PORTFOLIO DIVERSIFICATION LOWERS RISK
Basics

Problem. For simplicity, suppose that all risky assets have a standard deviation of 30% and all pairs of risky assets have a correlation coefficient of 40%. In this simple setting, consider a portfolio diversification strategy of investing in equally-weighted portfolios (e.g., put an equal about in each risky asset). As you increase the number of assets in your portfolio (that you are diversifying across), how much does this lower the risk of your portfolio?

Solution Strategy. Calculate the portfolio standard deviation of an equally-weighted portfolio as the number of assets increases. As a benchmark, compare with the portfolio standard deviation in the limiting case as the number of assets goes to infinity.

FIGURE 1. Spreadsheet Model of Portfolio Diversification Lowers Risk - Basics

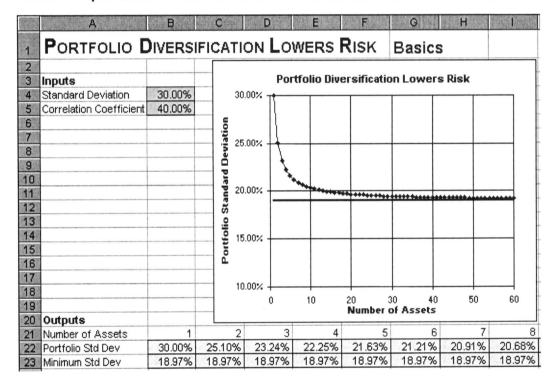

How To Build This Spreadsheet Model.

1. Enter The Inputs. Enter the inputs into the range **B4:B5**.

2. Number of Assets. Enter Number of Asset values **1,2, 3, 4, ...,60** in the range **B21:BI21**.

3. Portfolio Standard Deviation. The formula for the standard deviation of an equally-weighted portfolio in this simple setting is

$$\sqrt{\frac{1+\left(\text{Number of risky assets}-1\right)\cdot\text{Correlation Coefficient}}{\text{Number of risky assets}}}\cdot\text{Risky Asset Standard Deviation.}$$

Enter **=SQRT((1+(B21-1)*\$B\$5)/B21)*\$B\$4** in cell **B22** and copy the cell to the range **B22:BI22**.

4. Minimum Standard Deviation. In the limit as the number of assets goes to infinity, the formula above reduces to

$$\sqrt{\text{Correlation Coefficient}}\cdot\text{Risky Asset Standard Deviation,}$$

Enter **=SQRT(\$B\$5)*\$B\$4** in cell **B23** and copy the cell to the range **B23:BI23**.

5. Graph the Standard Deviations By The Number Of Risky Assets. Highlight the range **B21:BI23**. Next choose **Insert Chart** from the main menu. Select an **XY(Scatter)** chart type and make other selections to complete the Chart Wizard. Place the graph in the range **C2:I20**.

This graph shows how diversifying across many assets can reduce risk from 30% to as low as 18.97%. Most of the risk reduction is accomplished with a relatively small number of assets. Increasing the number of assets from one to ten accomplishes more that 85% of the potential risk reduction. Increasing to thirty assets accomplishes more than 95% of the potential risk reduction. In summary, very significant risk reduction can be accomplished by diversifying across thirty assets, but relatively little risk reduction is accomplished by increasing the number of assets further.

PORTFOLIO DIVERSIFICATION LOWERS RISK
International

Problem. There is a lot of evidence that international correlation coefficients are dramatically lower than local (same country) correlation coefficients. We can explore the benefits of international diversification by extending the Basics example. Suppose there are two countries and all risky assets in both countries have a standard deviation of 30%. All pairs of risky assets *within* the same country have a local correlation coefficient of 40%, but all pairs of risky assets *between* countries have an international correlation coefficient of 10%. Consider an international diversification strategy of investing half of your money in an equally-weighted portfolio in country 1 and the other half in an equally-weighted portfolio in country 2. As you increase the number of assets in your total portfolio, how much does this lower the risk of your portfolio?

Solution Strategy. Calculate the portfolio standard deviation of the internationally diversified portfolio as the number of assets increases. As a benchmark, compare with the international portfolio standard deviation in the limiting case as the number of assets goes to infinity.

FIGURE 1. Spreadsheet Model of Portfolio Diversification Lowers Risk - International.

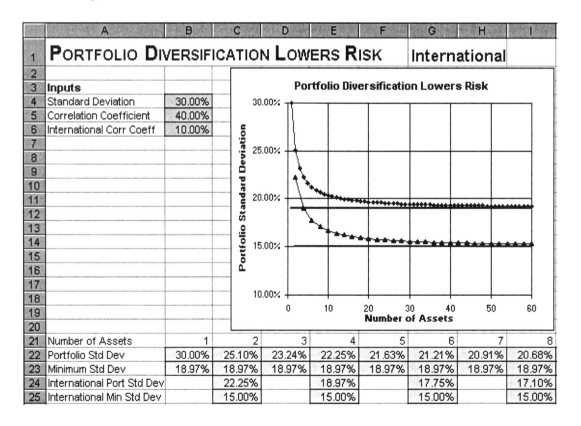

	A	B	C	D	E	F	G	H	I
1	PORTFOLIO DIVERSIFICATION LOWERS RISK						International		
2									
3	Inputs								
4	Standard Deviation	30.00%							
5	Correlation Coefficient	40.00%							
6	International Corr Coeff	10.00%							
7									
8									
9									
10									
11									
12									
13									
14									
15									
16									
17									
18									
19									
20									
21	Number of Assets	1	2	3	4	5	6	7	8
22	Portfolio Std Dev	30.00%	25.10%	23.24%	22.25%	21.63%	21.21%	20.91%	20.68%
23	Minimum Std Dev	18.97%	18.97%	18.97%	18.97%	18.97%	18.97%	18.97%	18.97%
24	International Port Std Dev		22.25%		18.97%		17.75%		17.10%
25	International Min Std Dev		15.00%		15.00%		15.00%		15.00%

How To Build This Spreadsheet Model.

1.Start with the Basics Spreadsheet. Open the spreadsheet that you created for Portfolio Diversification Lowers Risk - Basics and immediately save the spreadsheet under a new name using the **File Save As** command. Enter the international correlation coefficient **10.00%** in cell **B6**.

2.International Portfolio Standard Deviation. The formula for the standard deviation of the internationally diversified portfolio put half in an equally-weighted portfolio in each country is

$$\sqrt{\frac{1+\left(\# \text{ of assets} / 2 - 1\right) \cdot \text{Local Corr Coeff} + \left(\# \text{ of assets} / 2\right) \cdot \text{Intrnl Corr Coeff}}{\# \text{ of assets}}} \cdot \text{Asset Std Dev.}$$

Enter **=SQRT((2+(C21-2)*$B$5+C21*$B$6)/(2*C21))*$B$4** in cell **C24** and copy the cell to the range **D24:BI24**. Then delete the formula from all of cells that correspond to an odd number of assets (**D24, F24, H24, ..., BH24**), because you can't evenly divide an odd number of assets.

3.International Minimum Standard Deviation. In the limit as the number of assets goes to infinity, the formula above reduces to

$$\sqrt{\left(1/2\right) \cdot \text{Local Corr Coeff} + \left(1/2\right) \cdot \text{Intrnl Corr Coeff}} \cdot \text{Asset Std Dev.}$$

Enter **=SQRT(0.5*$B$5+0.5*$B$6)*$B$4** in cell **C25** and copy the cell to the range **D25:BI25**. Then delete the formula from all of cells that correspond to an odd number of assets (**D25, F25, H25, ..., BH25**), because you can't evenly divide an odd number of assets.

4.Add the International Standard Deviations To The Chart. Hover the cursor over the Chart and then click on the right mouse button. From the pop-up menu, select **Source Data**, edit the Data Range to read **=Sheet1!$B$21:$BI$25**, and click on **OK**. To fill in the gaps between even numbered observations, click on the Chart, then click on **Tools Options**, click on the **Chart** tab, click on the **Interpolated** radio button, and **OK**.

This graph shows how international diversification can significantly reduce risk beyond local (one country) diversification. In this example, local diversification reduces risk from 30% to as low as 18.57%, but international diversification can reduce risk as low as 15%. International diversification works by getting rid of some country-specific sources of risk. Again, most of the risk reduction is accomplished with a relatively small number of assets. Beyond 30 assets (15 in each country), there is not much risk reduction potential left.

LIFE-CYCLE FINANCIAL PLANNING
Basics

Problem. Develop a financial plan for investment and consumption over your life-cycle (from the present 'til your death). Suppose the inflation rate is 2.0% and the real return on a riskfree money market fund is 3.5%. Suppose that a risky diversified fund offers an average real return of 8.0% and a standard deviation of 17.0%, which is equivalent to the post-World War II average real return and standard deviation on a well-diversified portfolio of US stocks. Suppose that federal income taxes have five brackets with the following rates: 15.0%, 28.0%, 31.0%, 36.0%, and 39.6%. For current year, the upper cutoff on the first four brackets are $43,050 $104,050, $158,550, and $283,150 and these cutoffs are indexed to inflation. The state tax rate = 3.0%, federal FICA-SSI tax rate on salary up to $72,600 is 6.2%, and the federal FICA-Medicare tax rate on any level of salary is 1.45%. Suppose you are currently 25 years old and you expect to earn a salary next year of $70,000. You currently have $0 in a retirement account and plan to work through age 65. You will start receiving social security benefits at age 66. The current level of social security benefits is $15,480 per year and this is indexed to inflation. Explore the investment and consumption impacts over the life-cycle of the following *choice variables* :

• **Savings Percentage.** The percentage of your annual salary that you contribute to your retirement fund during your working years.

• **Risky Diversified Fund Percentage.** The percentage of your retirement fund that you put in the risky diversified fund (vs. the riskfree money market fund).

• **Withdrawal Percentage.** The percentage of your retirement fund that you withdraw each year to live on during your retirement years.

• **Real Growth Rate in Salary.** The real portion of the annual growth in your salary. You salary also increases with inflation.

Solution Strategy. Develop a spreadsheet model of investment and consumption on a year-by-year basis over an entire lifetime. You need to choose how to divide your salary between providing consumption now vs. savings (to provide for consumption in the future). Your savings are put in a tax-deferred retirement account and each year you need to decide what percentage to contribute to it (or withdraw from it). You avoid paying taxes on contributions to the retirement fund, but you suffer paying taxes when you withdraw from it. Salary less contributions plus withdraws gives you taxable income upon which you pay taxes. The after-tax income plus social security benefits provide for consumption each year. You need to choose what percentage of your retirement funds to invest in the risky diversified fund. The rest of your retirement funds will be invested in the riskfree money market fund and will grow at the riskfree rate. Investing in the risky diversified fund will give you a higher average returns than the riskfree money market fund, but also more risk. You also need to choose how fast to withdraw funds from your retirement account during your retirement years. A steady state withdraw policy is one that withdraws the average real increase in the retirement fund each year. This avoids touching the principal amount and allows it to grow at the rate of inflation. A steady state withdraw policy can be sustained indefinitely (i.e., no matter how long you live). For convenience, the spreadsheet analysis is carried out to age 90. How long will you live? Well, for today's US population of 65 year olds, average life expectancy is 82. To determine your individual life expectancy, add to (or subtract from) 82 based your individual health-conscious practices. Not smoking adds nine years. Aerobic exercising and getting seven to eight hours of sleep per night adds three years. A healthy diet

FIGURE 1. Spreadsheet Model for Life-Cycle Financial Planning - Basics.

	A	B	C	D	E	F	G
1	**LIFE-CYCLE FINANCIAL PLANNING**			**Basics**			
2							
3	**Inputs**						
4	Inflation Rate	2.0%					
5	Real Ret on Riskfree Money Market Fund	3.5%					
6	Ave Real Ret on Risky Diversified Fund	8.0%					
7	Std Dev of Risky Diversified Fund	0.0001%					
8	Federal Income Bracket 1 Tax Rate	15.0%					
9	Federal Income Bracket 2 Tax Rate	28.0%					
10	Federal Income Bracket 3 Tax Rate	31.0%					
11	Federal Income Bracket 4 Tax Rate	36.0%					
12	Federal Income Bracket 5 Tax Rate	39.6%					
13	Federal FICA-SSI Tax Rate on Salary	6.2%					
14	Federal FICA-Medicare Tax on Salary	1.45%					
15	State Income Tax Rate	3.0%					
16							
17	Date	0	1	2	3	4	5
18	Age	25	26	27	28	29	30
19	**Choice Variables**						
20	Savings Percentage		8.1%	8.1%	8.1%	8.1%	8.1%
21	Risky Diversified Fund Percentage		100.0%	100.0%	100.0%	100.0%	100.0%
22	Withdrawal Percentage		0.0%	0.0%	0.0%	0.0%	0.0%
23	Real Growth Rate in Salary			2.0%	2.0%	2.0%	2.0%
24							
25	**Random Variables**						
26	Real Return on Risky Diversified Fund		8.00%	8.00%	8.00%	8.00%	8.00%
27	Real Return on Your Retirement Fund		8.00%	8.00%	8.00%	8.00%	8.00%
28							
29	**Outputs**						
30	Salary		$70,000	$72,828	$75,770	$78,831	$82,016
31	Less Contribution To Retirement Fund		$5,670	$5,899	$6,137	$6,385	$6,643
32	Plus Withdrawal From Retirement Fund		$0	$0	$0	$0	$0
33	Taxable Income		$64,330	$66,929	$69,633	$72,446	$75,373
34	Less Taxes		$19,589	$20,497	$21,444	$22,416	$23,346
35	After-Tax Income		$44,741	$46,432	$48,189	$50,030	$52,027
36	Plus Social Security Benefits		$0	$0	$0	$0	$0
37	Consumption		$44,741	$46,432	$48,189	$50,030	$52,027
38							
39	Retirement Fund	$0	$5,670	$12,145	$19,516	$27,885	$37,361
40	Real Consumption in Current Dollars		$43,864	$44,629	$45,410	$46,220	$47,123
41	Difference in Real Consump (Post-Pre)	$340					
42	Social Security Benefit Level		$15,480	$15,790	$16,105	$16,427	$16,756
43	Federal Income Tax Bracket 1 Cutoff	$43,050	$43,911	$44,789	$45,685	$46,599	$47,531
44	Federal Income Tax Bracket 2 Cutoff	$104,050	$106,131	$108,254	$110,419	$112,627	$114,880
45	Federal Income Tax Bracket 3 Cutoff	$158,550	$161,721	$164,955	$168,255	$171,620	$175,052
46	Federal Income Tax Bracket 4 Cutoff	$283,150	$288,813	$294,589	$300,481	$306,491	$312,620
47	Federal FICA-SSI Wage Cap	$72,600	$74,052	$75,533	$77,044	$78,585	$80,156

Chart (rows 2-16, columns C-G): "Real Consumption Over The Life-Cycle" — y-axis "Real Consumption" from $0 to $200,000; x-axis "Age" from 25 to 85.

and maintaining a desirable weight based on your height adds three years. A thorough annual medical exam to catch cancer and other health problems early adds two years. The following six items add one year each: (1) daily aspirin to reduce fatal heart attacks, (2) preventing high blood pressure, (3) avoiding accidents, (4) getting immunized against pneumonia and influenza, (5) avoiding suicide and AIDS, and (6) avoiding heavy alcohol consumption. For the subset of future scientific/medical progress. For more information on the factors effecting longevity and the latest scientific/medical progress, visit http://members.aol.com/webstergc/Index.html

How To Build This Spreadsheet Model.

1.Inputs. Enter the *inputs* described in the problem into the range **B4:B15**, the cells **B18**, **C30**, **B39**, **C42**, and the range **B43:B47**. For the time being, enter **0.0001%** in cell **B7** as the standard deviation rather than 17%. Lock in the left column of titles by selecting the cell **B1** and clicking on **Window Freeze Panes**.

2.Date and Age. For the Date row, enter **0, 1, 2,..., 65** in the range **B17:BO17**. The easy way to do this is enter **0** in cell **B17**, **1** in cell **C17**, highlight the range **B17:C17**, put the cursor over the lower right corner of cell **C17** until it becomes a "plus" icon, and drag the cursor all the way across to cell **BO17**. For the Age row, enter **=B18+1** in cell **C18** and copy the cell to the range **D18:BO18**:

3.Choice Variables. Each year, starting with age 26 (column **C**) and continuing through age 90 (column **BO**), you need to make certain decisions. Each decision is called a choice variable. Enter initial values for the choice variables into the ranges **C20:BO22** and **D23:BO23**. **Figure 2** below shows the two steps involved in implementing retirement. (1) Enter **-100.0%** in cell **AQ23**,

FIGURE 2. Working Years vs. Retirement Years.

	A	AO	AP	AQ	AR	AS
17	Date	39	40	41	42	43
18	Age	64	65	66	67	68
19	**Choice Variables**					
20	Savings Percentage	8.1%	8.1%	0.0%	0.0%	0.0%
21	Risky Diversified Fund Percentage	100.0%	100.0%	50.0%	50.0%	50.0%
22	Withdrawal Percentage	0.0%	0.0%	5.9%	5.9%	5.9%
23	Real Growth Rate in Salary	2.0%	2.0%	-100.0%	0.0%	0.0%
24						
25	**Random Variables**					
26	Real Return on Risky Diversified Fund	8.00%	8.00%	8.00%	8.00%	8.00%
27	Real Return on Your Retirement Fund	8.00%	8.00%	5.75%	5.75%	5.75%
28						
29	**Outputs**					
30	Salary	$315,291	$328,028	$0	$0	$0
31	Less Contribution To Retirement Fund	$25,539	$26,570	$0	$0	$0
32	Plus Withdrawal From Retirement Fund	$0	$0	$234,156	$238,840	$243,616
33	Taxable Income	$289,752	$301,458	$234,156	$238,840	$243,616
34	Less Taxes	$93,959	$97,941	$59,984	$61,184	$62,407
35	After-Tax Income	$195,793	$203,517	$174,172	$177,656	$181,209
36	Plus Social Security Benefits	$0	$0	$34,180	$34,864	$35,561
37	Consumption	$195,793	$203,517	$208,353	$212,520	$216,770
38						
39	Retirement Fund	$3,600,092	$3,992,431	$4,072,285	$4,153,729	$4,236,810
40	Real Consumption in Current Dollars	$90,446	$92,171	$92,511	$92,511	$92,511
41	Difference in Real Consump (Post-Pre)					
42	Social Security Benefit Level	$32,853	$33,510	$34,180	$34,864	$35,561
43	Federal Income Tax Bracket 1 Cutoff	$93,192	$95,056	$96,957	$98,896	$100,874
44	Federal Income Tax Bracket 2 Cutoff	$225,242	$229,747	$234,341	$239,028	$243,809
45	Federal Income Tax Bracket 3 Cutoff	$343,220	$350,085	$357,086	$364,228	$371,513
46	Federal Income Tax Bracket 4 Cutoff	$612,947	$625,206	$637,711	$650,465	$663,474
47	Federal FICA-SSI Wage Cap	$157,160	$160,304	$163,510	$166,780	$170,116

which is the age 66 (first retirement year) Real Growth Rate in Salary. This causes the age 66 Salary in cell **AQ30** to drop to zero. (2) Given that you have no salary, you need to withdraw a percentage of the money in your retirement fund to live on. A Steady State Withdrawal Percentage = Average Real Return on the Retirement Fund * (1 + Inflation Rate) = (Risky Diversified Fund Percentage * Average Real Return on the Risk Diversified Fund + (1 - Risky Diversified Fund Percentage) * Real Return on the Riskfree Money Market Fund) * (1 + Inflation Rate). Enter **=(AQ21*$B$6+(1-AQ21)*$B$5)*(1+$B$4)** in cell **AQ22** and copy the cell to the range **AR22:BO22**. By the way, the last term "(1 + Inflation Rate)" takes care of the cross-product between (1 + real return) and (1 + inflation rate), so that the retirement fund can grow at the inflation rate.

As you adapt this model to your own situation, it is not necessary to go from full-time work to zero work. You could consider retiring to part-time work and then gradually tapering off. For example, you could drop to half-time work by entering **-50%** in your first retirement year and then enter **-100.0%** in the year that you stop working entirely.

4.Random Variables. Assume that the Real Return on the Risky Diversified Fund is normally distributed with the mean given in cell **B6** and the standard deviation given in cell **B7**. The Excel function **RAND()** generates a random variable with a uniform distribution over the interval from 0 to 1 (that is, an equal chance of getting any number between 0 and 1). To transform this uniformly distributed random variable into a normally distributed one, just place it inside the Excel function **NORMINV**.[1] Enter **=NORMINV(RAND(),$B$6,$B$7)** in cell **C26** and copy this cell to the range **D26:BO26**. The real return that you get depends on how much you have placed in risky vs. riskfree funds. Real Return on Your Retirement Fund = (Risky Diversified Fund Percentage) * (Real Return on Risky Diversified Fund) + (1 - Risky Diversified Fund Percentage) * (Real Return on Riskfree Money Market Fund). Enter **=C21*C26+(1-C21)*$B$5** in cell **C27** and copy this cell to the range **D27:BO27**.

5.Outputs. Here are the formulas for each row:

- **Salary** = Last Year's Salary * (1 + Inflation Rate) * (1 + Real Growth Rate in Salary) in working years Enter **=C30*(1+$B$4)*(1+D23)** in cell **D30** and copy the cell to the range **E30:BO30**.

- **Less Contribution To Retirement Fund** = (Savings Percentage) * (Salary). Enter **=C20*C30** in cell **C31** and copy the cell to the range **D31:BO31**.

- **Plus Withdrawal From Retirement Fund** = (Savings Percentage) * (Salary). Enter **=C22*B39** in cell **C32** and copy the cell to the range **D32:BO32**.

- **Taxable Income** = Salary - (Contribution To Retirement Fund) + (Withdrawal From Retirement Fund). Enter **=C30-C31+C32** in cell **C33** and copy the cell to the range **D33:BO33**.

- **Taxes** = (Bracket 1 Tax Rate) * MIN(Taxable Income, Bracket 1 Cutoff)

  + (Bracket 2 Tax Rate) * MAX(MIN(Taxable Income, Bracket 2 Cutoff) - Bracket 1 Cutoff, 0)

FIGURE 3. Old Age Years.

A	BK	BL	BM	BN	BO
17 Date	61	62	63	64	65
18 Age	86	87	88	89	90
19 **Choice Variables**					
20 Savings Percentage	0.0%	0.0%	0.0%	0.0%	0.0%
21 Risky Diversified Fund Percentage	50.0%	50.0%	50.0%	50.0%	50.0%
22 Withdrawal Percentage	5.9%	5.9%	5.9%	5.9%	5.9%
23 Real Growth Rate in Salary	0.0%	0.0%	0.0%	0.0%	0.0%
24					
25 **Random Variables**					
26 Real Return on Risky Diversified Fund	8.00%	8.00%	8.00%	8.00%	8.00%
27 Real Return on Your Retirement Fund	5.75%	5.75%	5.75%	5.75%	5.75%
28					
29 **Outputs**					
30 Salary	$0	$0	$0	$0	$0
31 Less Contribution To Retirement Fund	$0	$0	$0	$0	$0
32 Plus Withdrawal From Retirement Fund	$347,944	$354,903	$362,001	$369,241	$376,625
33 Taxable Income	$347,944	$354,903	$362,001	$369,241	$376,625
34 Less Taxes	$89,133	$90,916	$92,734	$94,589	$96,480
35 After-Tax Income	$258,811	$263,987	$269,267	$274,652	$280,145
36 Plus Social Security Benefits	$50,790	$51,806	$52,842	$53,899	$54,977
37 Consumption	$309,601	$315,793	$322,109	$328,551	$335,122
38					
39 Retirement Fund	$6,051,201	$6,172,222	$6,295,662	$6,421,572	$6,550,000
40 Real Consumption in Current Dollars	$92,511	$92,511	$92,511	$92,511	$92,511
41 Difference in Real Consump (Post-Pre)					
42 Social Security Benefit Level	$50,790	$51,806	$52,842	$53,899	$54,977
43 Federal Income Tax Bracket 1 Cutoff	$144,073	$146,955	$149,894	$152,892	$155,950
44 Federal Income Tax Bracket 2 Cutoff	$348,219	$355,183	$362,287	$369,533	$376,924
45 Federal Income Tax Bracket 3 Cutoff	$530,612	$541,224	$552,048	$563,089	$574,351
46 Federal Income Tax Bracket 4 Cutoff	$947,604	$966,556	$985,888	$1,005,605	$1,025,717
47 Federal FICA-SSI Wage Cap	$242,967	$247,826	$252,783	$257,838	$262,995

+ (Bracket 3 Tax Rate) * MAX(MIN(Taxable Income, Bracket 3 Cutoff) - Bracket 2 Cutoff, 0)

+ (Bracket 4 Tax Rate) * MAX(MIN(Taxable Income, Bracket 4 Cutoff) - Bracket 3 Cutoff, 0)

+ (Bracket 5 Tax Rate) * MAX(Taxable Income - Bracket 4 Cutoff, 0)

+ (Federal FICA-SSI Tax Rate) * MIN(Salary, Federal FICA-SSI Wage Cap)

+ (Federal FICA-Medicare Tax Rate) * Salary

+ (State Income Tax Rate) * Taxable Income

Enter **=$B$8*MIN(C33,C43) +$B$9*MAX(MIN(C33,C44) -C43,0) +$B$10*MAX (MIN (C33,C45) -C44,0) +$B$11*MAX(MIN(C33,C46)-C45,0) +$B$12*MAX(C33-C46,0) +$B$13*MIN(C30,C47) +$B$14*C30+$B$15*C33** in cell **C34** and copy the cell to the range **D34:BO34**.

- **After-Tax Income** = Taxable Income - Taxes. Enter **=C33-C34** in cell **C35** and copy the cell to the range **D35:BO35**.

- **Plus Social Security Benefits** = 0 in working years = Social Security Benefit Level in retirement year Enter **0** in cell **C36** and copy the cell to the range **D36:AP36**. Enter **=AQ42** in cell **AQ36** and copy the cell to the range **AR36:BO36**.

- **Consumption** = After-Tax Income + Social Security Benefits. Enter **=C35+C36** in cell **C37** and copy the cell to the range **D37:BO37**.

- **Retirement Fund** = Last Year's Retirement Fund * (1 + Inflation Rate) * (1 + Real Return on Your Retirement Fund) + Contribution to the Retirement Fund - Withdrawal from the Retirement Fund. Enter **=B39*(1+$B$4)*(1+C27)+C31-C32** in cell **C39** and copy the cell to the range **D39:BO39**.

- **Real Consumption** = (Nominal Consumption) / ((1 + Inflation Rate) ^ Number of periods) Enter **=C37/((1+$B$4)^C17)** in cell **C40** and copy the cell to the range **D40:BO40**.

- **Difference in Real Consumption (Post-Pre)** = Real Consumption in Post-Retirement - Real Consumption in Pre-Retirement. Enter **=AQ40-AP40** in cell **B41**.

- **Social Security Benefit Level** = Last Year's Social Security Benefit Level * (1 + Inflation Rate). Enter **=C42*(1+$B$4)** in cell **D42** and copy the cell to the range **E42:BO42**. To check your social security eligibility and benefit level, surf the Social Security Administration's web site www.ssa.gov/OACT/ANYPIA/ .

- **Federal Income Tax Bracket Cutoffs.** = Last Year's Federal Income Tax Bracket Cutoff * (1 + Inflation Rate). Enter **=B43*(1+$B$4)** in cell **C43** and copy the cell to the range **D43:BO46**.

- **Federal FICA-SSI Wage Cap.** = Last Year's Federal FICA-SSI Wage Cap * (1 + Inflation Rate). Enter **=B47*(1+$B$4)** in cell **C47** and copy the cell to the range **D47:BO47**.

6 Graph Real Consumption Over The Life-Cycle. Highlight the range **B18:BO18**, then hold down the Control button and (while still holding it down) select the range **B40:BO40**. Next choose **Insert Chart** from the main menu. Select an **XY(Scatter)** chart type and make other selections to complete the Chart Wizard. Place the graph in the range **C2:G16**.

7.Adjust Savings Percentage To Smooth Real Consumption Over The Life-Cycle. It doesn't make any sense to live like a king in your working years and the live in poverty in your retirement years. Similarly, it doesn't make sense to live in poverty in your working years and live like a king in your retirement years. The key idea is that you want to have a smooth pattern of real consumption over the life-cycle. The easiest way to get a smooth consumption pattern is to adjust the savings percentage. The easiest way to do this is to have a constant savings percentage during your working years by tying this savings percentage to a single cell and then manually adjust this cell. Enter **=C20** in cell **D20** and copy the cell to the range **E20:BO20**. Then manually adjust cell **C20** up or down in small increments until the Difference in Real Consumption (Post-Pre) in cell B41 is reasonably close to zero.

Looking at the big picture, the retirement fund starts at $0 and rises smoothly to $4,072,321 in the first retirement year and then increases at the rate of inflation each year after that. Focusing on the graph of real consumption over the life-cycle, we see that real consumption (in current dollars) starts out at $43,864 and rises smoothly to $92,511 at retirement and then stays constant at that level throughout retirement -- a comfortable lifestyle!

8.Adjust The Standard Deviation and View The Risk Involved. Now change the standard deviation to a realistic figure. Enter **17.0000%** in cell **B7**. The random variables in rows **26** and **27** will spring to life and the graph of real consumption over the life-cycle will reflect the high or low realizations of the risky diversified fund. Press the **F9** Recalculation key several times and you will see the real consumption rate dance all over the graph. **Figure 4** shows a low consumption case due to low real returns. **Figure 5** shows a medium consumption case due to medium real returns **Figure 6** shows a high consumption case due to high real returns.

FIGURE 4. A Low Consumption Case Due To Low Real Returns in the Risky Diversified Fund.

	A	B	C	D	E	F	G
1	LIFE-CYCLE FINANCIAL PLANNING			Basics			
2							
3	**Inputs**						
4	Inflation Rate	2.0%					
5	Real Ret on Riskfree Money Market Fund	3.5%					
6	Ave Real Ret on Risky Diversified Fund	8.0%					
7	Std Dev of Risky Diversified Fund	17.0000%					
8	Federal Income Bracket 1 Tax Rate	15.0%					
9	Federal Income Bracket 2 Tax Rate	28.0%					
10	Federal Income Bracket 3 Tax Rate	31.0%					
11	Federal Income Bracket 4 Tax Rate	36.0%					
12	Federal Income Bracket 5 Tax Rate	39.6%					
13	Federal FICA-SSI Tax Rate on Salary	6.2%					
14	Federal FICA-Medicare Tax on Salary	1.45%					
15	State Income Tax Rate	3.0%					
16							
17	Date	0	1	2	3	4	5
18	Age	25	26	27	28	29	30
19	**Choice Variables**						
20	Savings Percentage		8.1%	8.1%	8.1%	8.1%	8.1%
21	Risky Diversified Fund Percentage		100.0%	100.0%	100.0%	100.0%	100.0%
22	Withdrawal Percentage		0.0%	0.0%	0.0%	0.0%	0.0%
23	Real Growth Rate in Salary			2.0%	2.0%	2.0%	2.0%
24							
25	**Random Variables**						
26	Real Return on Risky Diversified Fund		-0.44%	22.99%	-20.34%	5.52%	6.95%
27	Real Return on Your Retirement Fund		-0.44%	22.99%	-20.34%	5.52%	6.95%
28							
29	**Outputs**						
30	Salary		$70,000	$72,828	$75,770	$78,831	$82,016
31	Less Contribution To Retirement Fund		$5,670	$5,899	$6,137	$6,385	$6,643
32	Plus Withdrawal From Retirement Fund		$0	$0	$0	$0	$0
33	Taxable Income		$64,330	$66,929	$69,633	$72,446	$75,373
34	Less Taxes		$19,589	$20,497	$21,444	$22,416	$23,346
35	After-Tax Income		$44,741	$46,432	$48,189	$50,030	$52,027
36	Plus Social Security Benefits		$0	$0	$0	$0	$0
37	Consumption		$44,741	$46,432	$48,189	$50,030	$52,027
38							
39	Retirement Fund	$0	$5,670	$13,012	$16,711	$24,371	$33,230
40	Real Consumption in Current Dollars		$43,864	$44,629	$45,410	$46,220	$47,123

FIGURE 5. A Medium Consumption Case Due To Medium Real Returns in the Risky Diversified Fund.

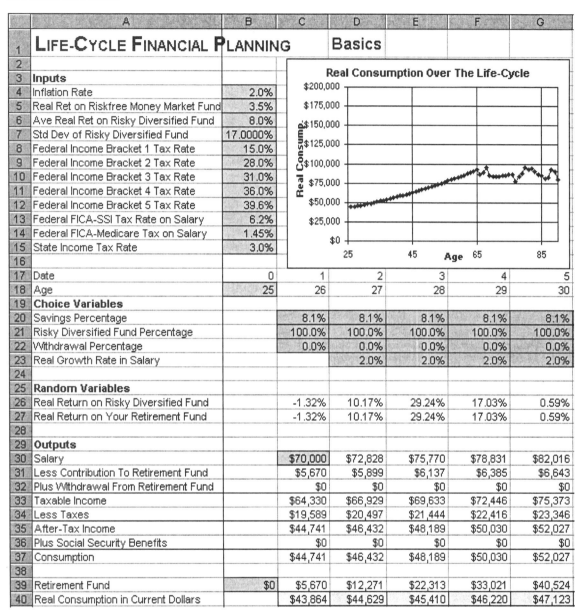

	A	B	C	D	E	F	G
1	LIFE-CYCLE FINANCIAL PLANNING		Basics				
2							
3	**Inputs**						
4	Inflation Rate	2.0%					
5	Real Ret on Riskfree Money Market Fund	3.5%					
6	Ave Real Ret on Risky Diversified Fund	8.0%					
7	Std Dev of Risky Diversified Fund	17.0000%					
8	Federal Income Bracket 1 Tax Rate	15.0%					
9	Federal Income Bracket 2 Tax Rate	28.0%					
10	Federal Income Bracket 3 Tax Rate	31.0%					
11	Federal Income Bracket 4 Tax Rate	36.0%					
12	Federal Income Bracket 5 Tax Rate	39.6%					
13	Federal FICA-SSI Tax Rate on Salary	6.2%					
14	Federal FICA-Medicare Tax on Salary	1.45%					
15	State Income Tax Rate	3.0%					
16							
17	Date	0	1	2	3	4	5
18	Age	25	26	27	28	29	30
19	**Choice Variables**						
20	Savings Percentage		8.1%	8.1%	8.1%	8.1%	8.1%
21	Risky Diversified Fund Percentage		100.0%	100.0%	100.0%	100.0%	100.0%
22	Withdrawal Percentage		0.0%	0.0%	0.0%	0.0%	0.0%
23	Real Growth Rate in Salary			2.0%	2.0%	2.0%	2.0%
24							
25	**Random Variables**						
26	Real Return on Risky Diversified Fund		-1.32%	10.17%	29.24%	17.03%	0.59%
27	Real Return on Your Retirement Fund		-1.32%	10.17%	29.24%	17.03%	0.59%
28							
29	**Outputs**						
30	Salary		$70,000	$72,828	$75,770	$78,831	$82,016
31	Less Contribution To Retirement Fund		$5,670	$5,899	$6,137	$6,385	$6,643
32	Plus Withdrawal From Retirement Fund		$0	$0	$0	$0	$0
33	Taxable Income		$64,330	$66,929	$69,633	$72,446	$75,373
34	Less Taxes		$19,589	$20,497	$21,444	$22,416	$23,346
35	After-Tax Income		$44,741	$46,432	$48,189	$50,030	$52,027
36	Plus Social Security Benefits		$0	$0	$0	$0	$0
37	Consumption		$44,741	$46,432	$48,189	$50,030	$52,027
38							
39	Retirement Fund	$0	$5,670	$12,271	$22,313	$33,021	$40,524
40	Real Consumption in Current Dollars		$43,864	$44,629	$45,410	$46,220	$47,123

These three graphs are "representative" of the risk you face from investing in the risky diversified fund. In the low case, real consumption drops to about $40,000. In the medium case, real consumption fluctuates between $75,000 and $100,000. In the high case, real consumption fluctuates between $125,000 and $160,000. Clearly, there is substantial risk from being so heavily exposed to the risky diversified fund.

There is a direct connection between risk and return. A high percentage in the risky diversified fund percentage gives you a high average return and high risk. Whereas a low percentage in the risky diversified fund percentage gives you a low average return and low risk. The choice is up to you.

FIGURE 6. A High Consumption Case Due To High Real Returns in the Risky Diversified Fund.

[1] The "Transformation Method" for converting a uniform random variable x into some other random variable y based on a cumulative distribution F is $y(x) = F^{-1}(x)$. See Press, W., B. Flannery, S. Teukolsky, and W. Vetterling, 1987, Numerical Recopies: The Art of Scientific Computing, Cambridge University Press, chapter on Random Numbers, subsection on the Transformation Method, page 201.

LIFE-CYCLE FINANCIAL PLANNING
Problems

Problems To Build And Use The Spreadsheet Models

1.Suppose the inflation rate is 2.4% and the real return on a riskfree money market fund is 3.8%. Suppose that a risky diversified fund offers an average real return of 7.2% and a standard deviation of 19.3%. Suppose that federal income taxes have five brackets with the following rates: 15.0%, 28.0%, 31.0%, 36.0%, and 39.6%. For current year, the upper cutoff on the first four brackets are $43,050, $104,050, $158,550, and $283,150 and these cutoffs are indexed to inflation.The state tax rate = 4.5%, federal FICA-SSI tax rate on salary up to $72,600 is 6.2%, and the federal FICA-Medicare tax rate on any level of salary is 1.45%. Suppose you are currently 35 years old and you expect to earn a salary next year of $90,000. You currently have $40,000 in a retirement account and plan to work through age 70. You will start receiving social security benefits at age 71. The current level of social security benefits is $15,480 per year and this is indexed to inflation. Build the **Life-Cycle Financial Planning - Basics** model and use it to develop a financial plan for investment and consumption over your life-cycle.

Problems To Extend The Spreadsheet Models.

2.Extend the **Life-Cycle Financial Planning - Basics** model by converting the spreadsheet into a Dynamic Chart by adding spinners to drive the inputs. See **Black Scholes Option Pricing - Dynamic Chart** for details on how to implement spinners. After you click on the spinners to change the inputs, then adjust the Savings Percentage to have a smooth consumption pattern.

DIVIDEND DISCOUNT MODELS
Two Stage

Problem. Given the historical data, we can see that over last two years Hot Prospects Inc. has generated a very high real Return On Investment (Real ROI) of 22.3% and 20.7%. Over the last three years, its dividends per share has increased rapidly from $5.10 to $5.84 to $6.64. As the competition catches up over the next five years, the Hot Prospects Real ROI is expected to gradually slow down. The long-run forecast calls for the firm's Real ROI to match the firm's real discount rate (Real k), which is 9.0% per year. Hot Prospects follows a policy of retaining 50.0% of its earnings and paying out the rest as dividends. Going forward, the inflation rate is expected to be 3.0% per year indefinitely. What is the firm's intrinsic value / share?

Solution Strategy. Construct a two-stage discounted dividend model. In stage one, explicitly forecast the firm's dividend over a five-year horizon. In stage two, forecast the firm's dividend from year six to infinity and calculate it's continuation value as the present value of this constant growth annuity. Then, discount the future dividends and the date 5 continuation value back to the present to get the intrinsic value per share.

FIGURE 1. Spreadsheet for Dividend Discount Models - Two Stage.

	A	B	C	D	E	F	G	H	I	J
1	**DIVIDEND DISCOUNT MODELS**			**Two Stage**						
2										
3	**Inputs**									
4	Inflation Rate	3.0%								
5	Real Discount Rate (Real k)	9.0%								
6	Earnings Retention Rate	50.0%								
7										
8	**Outputs**									Stage 2:
9	Nominal Discount Rate (k)	12.3%								Infinite
10							Stage 1: Explicit Forecast			Horizon
11			Historical Data				Horizon (ROI > k)			(ROI = k)
12	Period	-2	-1	0	1	2	3	4	5	6
13	Inflation Rate		2.8%	3.1%	3.0%	3.0%	3.0%	3.0%	3.0%	3.0%
14	Real Return on Investment (Real ROI)		22.3%	20.7%	19.0%	17.0%	15.0%	13.0%	11.0%	9.0%
15	Nominal Return on Investment (ROI)		25.7%	24.4%	22.6%	20.5%	18.5%	16.4%	14.3%	12.3%
16	Real Growth Rate in Dividend (Real g)		11.2%	10.4%	9.5%	8.5%	7.5%	6.5%	5.5%	4.5%
17	Nominal Growth Rate in Dividend (g)		14.5%	13.7%	12.8%	11.8%	10.7%	9.7%	8.7%	7.6%
18	Nominal Dividend / Share	$5.10	$5.84	$6.64	$7.49	$8.37	$9.27	$10.17	$11.05	$11.89
19	Continuation Value / Share								$256.51	
20	Sum of Future Div. & Cont. Value/Shr				$7.49	$8.37	$9.27	$10.17	$267.56	
21	PV of Future Div. & Cont. Value / Shr				$6.67	$6.64	$6.55	$6.40	$150.00	
22	Intrinsic Value / Share			$176.26						

How To Build This Spreadsheet Model

1. Inputs. Enter the inflation rate, real discount rate, and earnings retention rate into the range **B4:B6**. Enter the historical data in the range **C13:D18** and the cell **B18**. Input the projected inflation rate by entering **=$B$4** in cell **E13** and copy the cell to the range **F13:J13**.

2.Calculate The Nominal Discount Rate. The Nominal Discount Rate = (1 + Inflation Rate) * (1 + Real Discount Rate) - 1. Enter **=(1+B4)*(1+B5)-1** in cell **B9**.

3.Forecast Future Real and Nominal ROI. In the long-run, the firm's Real ROI is forecast to equal the firm's real discount rate. Enter **=B5** in cell **J14**. Given the Real ROI of 20.7% on date 0 and a forecast of 9.0% per year starting in year 6, forecast the intermediate years by entering a smooth declining pattern, such as **19.0%**, **17.0%**, **15.0%**, etc. from date 1 to date 5 in the range **E14:I14**. For date 6, enter **=B5** in cell **J14**. Calculate the Nominal Return On Investment (ROI) = (1 + Inflation Rate) * (1 + Real ROI) - 1. Enter **=(1+E13)*(1+E14)-1** in cell **E15** and copy the cell to the range **F15:J15**.

4.Real and Nominal Growth Rate in Dividends. Calculate the Real Growth Rate in Dividend (Real g) = (Real ROI) * (Earnings Retention Rate). Enter **=E14*$B$6** in cell **E16** and copy the cell to the range **F16:J16**. Calculate the Nominal Growth Rate in Dividend (g) = (1 + Inflation Rate) (1 + Real g) - 1. Enter **=(1+$B$4)*(1+E16)-1** in cell **E17** and copy the cell to the range **F17:J17**.

5.Nominal Dividend / Share. Calculate the Date t Nominal Dividend = (Date t-1 Nominal Dividend) * (1 + Date t Nominal Growth Rate in Dividend). Enter **=D18*(1+E17)** in cell **E18** and copy the cell to the range **F18:J18**.

6.Date 5 Continuation Value. The Date 5 Continuation Value is the present value of the stream of dividends from date 6 to infinity. Using the present value of an infinitely growing annuity formula, calculate Date 5 Continuation Value = (Date 6 Dividend) / (Nominal Discount Rate - Date 6 Nominal Growth Rate in Dividends). Enter **=J18/(B9-J17)** in cell **I19**.

7.Sum and PV of Future Dividends and the Continuation Value / Share. On each date, sum the future dividend and continuation value / share. Enter **=SUM(E18:E19)** in cell **E20** and copy the cell to the range **F20:J20**. Calculate the Present Value of the Future Dividend and Continuation Value / Share = (Date t Sum) / ((1 + Nominal Discount Rate) ^ t). Enter **=E20/((1+$B$9)^E12)** in cell **E21** and copy it across the range **F21:I21**.

8.Intrinsic Value Per Share. Sum the PV of Future Dividends and Continuation Value. Enter **=SUM(E21:I21)** in cell **D22**.

Hot Prospects Inc. is estimated to have an intrinsic value per share of $176.26.

DIVIDEND DISCOUNT MODELS
Dynamic Chart

Problem. How sensitive is the Intrinsic Value to changes in: (1) the Inflation Rate, (2) Earnings Retention Rate, and (3) Real Discount Rate (k)? Said differently, how important is it to be very accurate in forecasting these three inputs?

Solution Strategy. First, we vary the Real Discount Rate input and use Excel's **Data Table** feature to generate the corresponding Intrinsic Value / Share outputs. Second, we construct a **Dynamic Chart** by graphing the Data Table inputs and outputs and by adding spinners to the Inflation Rate and Earnings Retention Rate inputs.

FIGURE 1. Spreadsheet for Dividend Discount Models - Dynamic Chart.

	A	B	C	D	E	F	G	H	I	J
1	**DIVIDEND DISCOUNT MODELS**			**Dynamic Chart**						
2										
3	**Inputs**									
4	Inflation Rate	3.0%		6						
5	Earnings Retention Rate	50.0%		5						
6										
7										
8										
9										
10										
11										
12										
13										
14	**Outputs**									
15	Real Discount Rate (Real k)	9.0%	7.0%	8.0%	9.0%	10.0%	11.0%	12.0%		
16	Intrinsic Value / Share	$176	$235	$202	$176	$156	$139	$125		
17										
18										Stage 2:
19	Nominal Discount Rate (k)	12.3%								Infinite
20						Stage 1: Explicit Forecast				Horizon
21			Historical Data			Horizon (ROI > k)				(ROI = k)
22	Period	-2	-1	0	1	2	3	4	5	6
23	Inflation Rate		2.8%	3.1%	3.0%	3.0%	3.0%	3.0%	3.0%	3.0%
24	Real Return on Investment (Real ROI)		22.3%	20.7%	19.0%	17.0%	15.0%	13.0%	11.0%	9.0%
25	Nominal Return on Investment (ROI)		25.7%	24.4%	22.6%	20.5%	18.5%	16.4%	14.3%	12.3%
26	Real Growth Rate in Dividend (Real g)		11.2%	10.4%	9.5%	8.5%	7.5%	6.5%	5.5%	4.5%
27	Nominal Growth Rate in Dividend (g)		14.5%	13.7%	12.8%	11.8%	10.7%	9.7%	8.7%	7.6%
28	Nominal Dividend / Share	$5.10	$5.84	$6.64	$7.49	$8.37	$9.27	$10.17	$11.05	$11.89
29	Continuation Value / Share								$256.51	
30	Sum of Future Div. & Cont. Value/Shr				$7.49	$8.37	$9.27	$10.17	$267.56	
31	PV of Future Div. & Cont. Value / Shr				$6.67	$6.64	$6.55	$6.40	$150.00	
32	Intrinsic Value / Share			$176.26						

82

How To Build This Spreadsheet Model.

1.Open the Two Stage Spreadsheet and Move A Few Things. Open the spreadsheet that you created for Dividend Discount Models - Two Stage and immediately save the spreadsheet under a new name using the **File Save As** command. Insert ten rows above the **Outputs**, by selecting the range **A8:A17** and clicking on **Insert Rows**. Move The Label "Outputs," by selecting the cell **A18**, clicking on **Edit Cut**, selecting the cell **A14** and clicking on **Edit Paste**. Using the same steps, move the range **A5:B5** to the range **A15:B15** and move the range **A6:B6** to the range **A5:B5**.

2.Increase Row Height for the Spinners. Select the range **A4:A5**. Then click on **Format Row Height** from the main menu. Enter a height of **30** and click on **OK**.

3.Display the Forms Toolbar. Select **View Toolbars Forms** from the main menu.

4.Create the Spinners. Look for the up-arrow / down-arrow button on the Forms toolbar (which will display the word "Spinner" if you hover the cursor over it) and click on it. Then draw the box for a spinner from the upper left corner of cell **C4** down to the lower right corner of the cell. Then a spinner appears in the cell **C4**. Right click on the spinner (press the right mouse button while the cursor is above the spinner) and a small menu pops up. Click on Copy. Then select the cell **C5** and click on Paste. This creates an identical spinner in cell **C5**. You now have two spinners down column **C**.

5.Create The Cell Links. Right click on the first spinner in the cell **C4** and a small menu pops up. Click on **Format Control** and a dialog box pops up. Enter the cell link **D4** in the **Cell link** edit box and click on **OK**. Repeat this procedure for the other spinner. Link the spinner in cell **C5** to cell **D5**. Click on the up-arrows and down-arrows of the spinners to see how they change the values in the linked cells.

6.Create Scaled Inputs. The values in the linked cells are always integers, but they can be scaled appropriately to the problem at hand. In cell **B4**, enter **=D4/200**. In cell **B5**, enter **=D5/10**.

7.Enter Real Discount Rate Values. In the range **C15:H15**, enter the values **7%**, **8%**, **9%**, **10%**, **11%**, and **12%**.

8.Create A Data Table To Calculate Intrinsic Value / Share. Use Excel's Data Table feature to calculate the Intrinsic Value / Share for each corresponding Real Discount Rate. Specify the output cell by entering **=D32** in cell **B16**. Select the range **B15:H16**, click on **Data Table**, enter **$B$15** in the **Row Input Cell** box, and click on **OK**.

9.Graph the Infinitely-long Rate and Yield to Maturity. Select the range **C15:H16**, then click on **Insert Chart** from the main menu. Select an **XY(Scatter)** chart type and make other selections to complete the Chart Wizard. Place the graph in the range **E2:J13**.

The Data Table and the graph indicate that decreasing the Real Discount Rate from 12% to 7% causes the Intrinsic Value / Share to jump from $125 / Share to $235 / Share. Thus, the Intrinsic

Rate causes no change at all in the Intrinsic Value / Share. This makes sense because the Inflation Rate contributes equally to the Nominal Return on Investment and to the Nominal Discount Rate. The two effects cancel each other out, leaving zero net impact on Intrinsic Value / Share. Clicking on the spinner for the Earnings Retention Rate causes a huge movement in the Intrinsic Value / Share. Hence, it is important to be as accurate as possible about both the Real Discount Rate and the Earnings Retention Rates.

DIVIDEND DISCOUNT MODELS
Problems

Problems To Build And Use The Spreadsheet Models

1. Suppose that a firm has generated a real Return On Investment (Real ROI) of 14.6% and 11.9% of the last two year, while the inflation rate as been 3.5% and 2.4%, respectively. Over the last three years, the firm's dividends per share have increased from $15.92 to $16.23 to $17.36. Over the next five years, the firm's Real ROI is expected to gradually slow down. The long-run forecast calls for the firm's Real ROI to match the firm's real discount rate (Real k), which is 6.2% per year. The firm follows a policy of retaining 34.0% of its earnings and paying out the rest as dividends. Going forward, the inflation rate is expected to be 4.1% per year indefinitely. Build the **Dividend Discount Models - Two Stage** model and use it to determine the firm's intrinsic value / share.

2. Build the **Dividend Discount Models - Dynamic Chart** model and use it to perform instant experiments on whether changing various inputs causes an increase or decrease in the firm's intrinsic value / share and by how much.

(a.) What happens when the inflation rate is increased?

(b.) What happens when the earnings retention rate is increased?

OPTION PAYOFFS AND PROFITS
Basics

Problem. A call option has an exercise price of $40.00 and a option price of $5.00. A put option has the same exercise price and option price. Graph the option payoffs and profits for buying or selling a call option and for buying or selling a put option.

Solution Strategy. We will create a switch that can be used to select buying or selling an option and another switch for a call vs. a put. For a range of stock prices at maturity, calculate the corresponding option payoffs and profits. Then graph it.

FIGURE 1. Spreadsheet Model of Option Payoffs and Profits - Basics

	A	B	C	D	E	F	G	H	I
1	OPTION PAYOFFS AND PROFITS				Basics		Buy	Call	
2									
3	Inputs								
4	Buy or Sell: 1 = Buy, -1 = Sell	1							
5	Option Type: 1=Call, 2=Put	1							
6	Exercise Price	$40.00							
7	Option Price	$5.00							
8									
21	Outputs								
22	Stock Price At Maturity	$0.00	$8.00	$16.00	$24.00	$32.00	$40.00	$48.00	$56.00
23	Option Payoff	$0.00	$0.00	$0.00	$0.00	$0.00	$0.00	$8.00	$16.00
24	Option Profit	-$5.00	-$5.00	-$5.00	-$5.00	-$5.00	-$5.00	$3.00	$11.00

How To Build This Spreadsheet Model.

1.Enter The Inputs. Enter **1** in cell **B4**. This will serve as a switch with **1** for Buying and. **-1** for Selling.Ê Enter **1** in cell **B5**. This will serve as a switch with **1** for a Call and **2** for a Put. To highlight which case is being considered, enter **=IF($B$4=1,"Buy","Sell")** in cell **G1** and **=IF($B$5=1,"Call","Put")** in cell **H1** Enter the other inputs into the range **B6:B7**.

86

2.Enter Stock Price At Maturity. Enter Stock Price At Maturity values **$0.00**, **$8.00**, **$16.00**, **$24.00**, **...**, **$80.00** in the range **B22:L22**.

3.Option Payoff. The formulas for option payoffs are:

- For a Call, the Payoff At Maturity = Max (Stock Price At Maturity - Exercise Price, 0).

- For a Put, the Payoff At Maturity = Max (Exercise Price - Stock Price At Maturity, 0).

We need to multiply these payoffs by the Buy or Sell switch in cell **B4**. Enter **=IF ($B$5=1,$B$4*MAX(B22-$B$6,0),$B$4*MAX($B$6-B22,0))** in cell **B23** and copy this cell to the range **C23:L23**.

4.Option Profit. The formula for an Option Profit = Option Payoff - (Buy or Sell switch) * (Option Price). Enter **=B23-$B$4*$B$7** in cell **B24** and copy this cell to the range **C24:L24**.

5.Graph the Option Payoffs and Profits. Highlight the range **B22:L24**. Next choose **Insert Chart** from the main menu. Select an **XY(Scatter)** chart type and make other selections to complete the Chart Wizard. Place the graph in the range **C2:I21**.

The graph displays the "hockey stick" payoffs and profits that characterize options. Change the switches between buy vs. sell and call vs. put to see all four graphs.

OPTION PAYOFFS AND PROFITS
Problems

Problems To Build And Use The Spreadsheet Models

1. A call option has an exercise price of $32.54 and a option price of $4.71. A put option has the same exercise price and option price. Build the **Option Payoffs and Profits - Basics** model and use it to graph the option payoffs and profits for buying or selling a call option and for buying or selling a put option.

2. A call option has an exercise price of $18.23 and a option price of $2.96. A put option has the same exercise price and option price. Build the **Option Payoffs and Profits - Basics** model and use it to graph the option payoffs and profits for buying or selling a call option and for buying or selling a put option.

OPTION TRADING STRATEGIES
Two Assets

Problem. There are three types of trading strategies involving options: (1) strategies involving a single option and a stock, (2) spreads involving options of one type (i.e., two or more calls or two or more puts), and (3) combinations involving both call(s) and put(s). Construct a chart that can show all of the trading strategies involving two assets.

Solution Strategy. We will create ranges for first asset inputs and for second asset inputs. Then calculate first asset profit, second asset profit, total profit, exercise price lines, and graph them.

FIGURE 1. Spreadsheet Model of Option Trading Strategies - Two Assets.

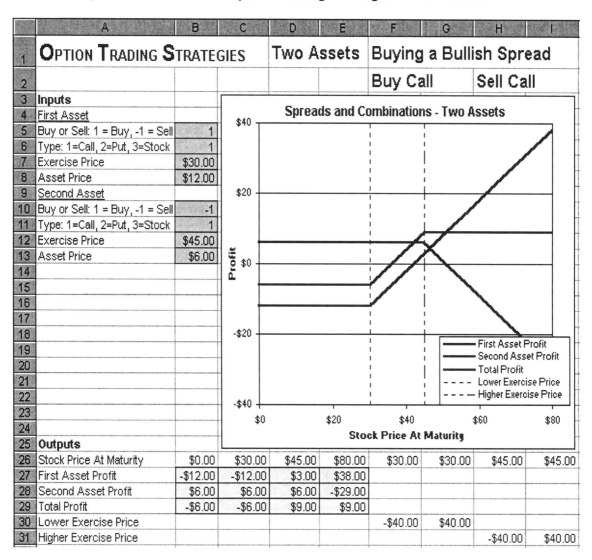

	A	B	C	D	E	F	G	H	I
1	**Option Trading Strategies**			**Two Assets**		**Buying a Bullish Spread**			
2						**Buy Call**		**Sell Call**	
3	Inputs								
4	First Asset								
5	Buy or Sell: 1 = Buy, -1 = Sell	1							
6	Type: 1=Call, 2=Put, 3=Stock	1							
7	Exercise Price	$30.00							
8	Asset Price	$12.00							
9	Second Asset								
10	Buy or Sell: 1 = Buy, -1 = Sell	-1							
11	Type: 1=Call, 2=Put, 3=Stock	1							
12	Exercise Price	$45.00							
13	Asset Price	$6.00							
14									
15									
16									
17									
18									
19									
20									
21									
22									
23									
24									
25	Outputs								
26	Stock Price At Maturity	$0.00	$30.00	$45.00	$80.00	$30.00	$30.00	$45.00	$45.00
27	First Asset Profit	-$12.00	-$12.00	$3.00	$38.00				
28	Second Asset Profit	$6.00	$6.00	$6.00	-$29.00				
29	Total Profit	-$6.00	-$6.00	$9.00	$9.00				
30	Lower Exercise Price					-$40.00	$40.00		
31	Higher Exercise Price							-$40.00	$40.00

89

How To Build This Spreadsheet Model.

1.Enter The Inputs. For the First Asset, enter **1** in cell **B5**. This will serve as a switch with **1** for Buying and. **-1** for Selling. Also for the First Asset, enter **1**in cell **B6**. This will serve as a switch with **1** for a Call, **2** for a Put, and **3** for a Stock. To highlight the First Asset, enter **=IF(B5=1,"Buy ","Sell ")&IF(B6=1,"Call",IF(B6=2,"Put","Stock"))** in cell **F2**. Enter the other First Asset inputs into the range **B7:B8**. Create the Second Asset inputs by copying the range **B5:B8** to the cell **B10** and highlight it by entering **=IF(B10=1,"Buy ","Sell ")&IF(B11=1, "Call", IF(B11=2, "Put", "Stock"))** in cell **H2**.

2.Enter Stock Price At Maturity. Enter Stock Price At Maturity value **$0.00** in cell **B26**, the lower exercise price **=IF(B7<B12,B7,B12)** in cell **C26**, the higher exercise price **=IF(B7>B12,B7,B12)** in cell **D26**, and **$80.00** in cell **E26**. Reference the lower exercise price **=$C$26** in **F26** and copy the cell to the cell **G26**. Reference the higher exercise price **=$D$26** in **H26** and copy the cell to the cell **I26**.

3.Asset Profit. The formulas for asset profits are:

- For a Call, the Profit = Max (Stock Price At Maturity - Exercise Price, 0) - Asset Price.

- For a Put, the Profit = Max (Exercise Price - Stock Price At Maturity, 0) - Asset Price.

- For a Stock, the Profit = Stock Price At Maturity - Asset Price

We need to multiply these profits by the First Asset Buy or Sell switch in cell **B5** or by the corresponding Second Asset Buy or Sell switch in cell **B10**. For the First Asset, Enter **=IF ($B$6=1,$B$5*(MAX(B26-$B$7,0)-$B$8) ,IF($B$6=2,$B$5* (MAX($B$7-B26,0)-$B$8), $B$5* (B26-$B$8)))** in cell **B27** and copy this cell to the range **C27:E27**. For the Second Asset, Enter **=IF($B$11=1,$B$10* (MAX(B26-$B$12,0)-$B$13), IF($B$11=2,$B$10* (MAX($B$12-B26,0)-$B$13) ,$B$10*(B26-$B$8)))** in cell **B28** and copy this cell to the range **C28:E28**.

4.Total Profit. The Total Profit = First Asset Profit + Second Asset Profit. Enter **=B27+B28** in cell **B29** and copy this cell to the range **C29:E29**.

5.Exercise Price Lines. When each asset is an option, it is convenient to have vertical lines on the graph at the corresponding exercise price. To do this enter **-40** in cell **F30**, **=IF (B6=3,-40,40)** in cell **G30**, **-40** in cell **H31**, **=IF(B11=3,-40,40)** in cell **H32**.

6.Graph the Asset Profits and Exercise Prices. Highlight the range **B26:I31**. Next choose **Insert Chart** from the main menu. Select an **XY(Scatter)** chart type and make other selections to complete the Chart Wizard. Place the graph in the range **C3:I25**.

FIGURE 2. Table of Option Trading Strategies.

	J	K	L
1			
2	Low-High:	Buy Call, Sell Call, Sell Call, Buy Call	
3			
4	Yes	Buying a Butterfly Spread	
5	No	Writing a Butterfly Spread	
6	No	Other Strategies	

7.(Optional) Add An Option Trading Strategy Label. As a nice extra touch, add a label in cell **F1** which identifies the type of option trading strategy. Here are the steps to accomplish this:

- **Two asset label.** Combine the labels in **F2** and **H2** starting with the asset which has the lowest exercise price. Enter **=IF(B7<B12,F2&", "&H2,H2&", "&F2)** in cell **K2**.

- **Buying a Covered Call.** Test for Buy Stock and Sell Call. Enter: **=IF(OR($K$2= "Buy Stock, Sell Call", $K$2= "Sell Call, Buy Stock"), "Yes","No")** in cell **J4**.

- **Writing a Covered Call.** Test for Sell Stock and Buy Call. Enter: **=IF(OR($K$2= "Sell Stock, Buy Call", $K$2= "Buy Call, Sell Stock"), "Yes","No")** in cell **J5**.

- **Buying a Protected Put.** Test for Buy Stock and Buy Put. Enter: **=IF(OR($K$2= "Buy Stock, Buy Put", $K$2= "Buy Put, Buy Stock"), "Yes","No")** in cell **J6**.

- **Writing a Protected Put.** Test for Sell Stock and Sell Put. Enter: **=IF(OR($K$2= "Sell Stock, Sell Put", $K$2="Sell Put, Sell Stock"), "Yes","No")** in cell **J7**.

- **Buying a Bullish Spread.** Test for Buy Call Low and Sell Call High or Buy Put Low and Sell Put High. Enter **=IF(OR($K$2= "Buy Call, Sell Call", $K$2="Buy Put, Sell Put"), "Yes","No")** in cell **J8**.

- **Buying a Bearish Spread.** Test for Sell Call Low and Buy Call High or Sell Put Low and Buy Put High. Enter **=IF(OR($K$2= "Sell Call, Buy Call", $K$2="Sell Put, Buy Put"), "Yes","No")** in cell **J9**.

- **Buying a Straddle.** Test for Buy Call and Buy Put and the same exercise price. In cell **J10**, enter **=IF(AND(OR($K$2= "Buy Call, Buy Put", $K$2="Buy Put, Buy Call"), $B$7=$B$12), "Yes","No")**.

- **Writing a Straddle.** Test for Buy Call and Buy Put and the same exercise price. In cell **J11**, enter **=IF(AND(OR($K$2= "Sell Call, Sell Put", $K$2="Sell Put, Sell Call"), $B$7=$B$12), "Yes","No")**.

- **Buying a Strangle.** Test for Buy Put Low and Buy Call High. Enter **=IF(OR($K$2= "Buy Put, Buy Call"),"Yes","No")** in cell **J12**.

- **Buying a Strangle.** Test for Sell Put Low and Sell Call High. Enter **=IF(OR($K$2= "Sell Put, Sell Call"), "Yes","No")** in cell **J13**.

- **Other Strategies.** Test the range **J4:J13** for "Yes" cases. Enter **=IF(COUNTIF (J4:J13, "=Yes")>0, "No","Yes")** in cell **J14**.

- **Option Trading Strategy Label.** Determine which type of option trading strategy applies by looking for "Yes" in the range **J4:J14** using the **VLOOKUP** function. Enter **=VLOOKUP ("Yes",J4:K14,2,FALSE)** in cell **F1**.

Incidentally in case you're wondering, Writing a Bullish Spread is the same as Buying a Bearish Spread. Similarly, Writing a Bearish Spread is the same as Buying a Bullish Spread.

OPTION TRADING STRATEGIES
Four Assets

Problem. Construct a chart that can show the trading strategies which involve four assets.

Solution Strategy. We will expand the input ranges to include a place for third asset inputs and fourth asset inputs. Then expand the calculations to include third asset profit, fourth asset profit, total profit, exercise price lines, and graph them.

FIGURE 1. Spreadsheet Model of Option Trading Strategies - Four Assets.

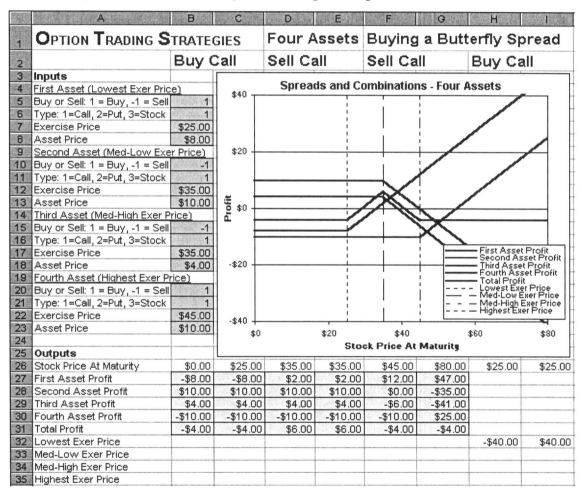

	A	B	C	D	E	F	G	H	I
1	**OPTION TRADING STRATEGIES**			**Four Assets**		**Buying a Butterfly Spread**			
2		**Buy Call**		**Sell Call**		**Sell Call**		**Buy Call**	
3	**Inputs**								
4	First Asset (Lowest Exer Price)								
5	Buy or Sell: 1 = Buy, -1 = Sell	1							
6	Type: 1=Call, 2=Put, 3=Stock	1							
7	Exercise Price	$25.00							
8	Asset Price	$8.00							
9	Second Asset (Med-Low Exer Price)								
10	Buy or Sell: 1 = Buy, -1 = Sell	-1							
11	Type: 1=Call, 2=Put, 3=Stock	1							
12	Exercise Price	$35.00							
13	Asset Price	$10.00							
14	Third Asset (Med-High Exer Price)								
15	Buy or Sell: 1 = Buy, -1 = Sell	-1							
16	Type: 1=Call, 2=Put, 3=Stock	1							
17	Exercise Price	$35.00							
18	Asset Price	$4.00							
19	Fourth Asset (Highest Exer Price)								
20	Buy or Sell: 1 = Buy, -1 = Sell	1							
21	Type: 1=Call, 2=Put, 3=Stock	1							
22	Exercise Price	$45.00							
23	Asset Price	$10.00							
24									
25	**Outputs**								
26	Stock Price At Maturity	$0.00	$25.00	$35.00	$35.00	$45.00	$80.00	$25.00	$25.00
27	First Asset Profit	-$8.00	-$8.00	$2.00	$2.00	$12.00	$47.00		
28	Second Asset Profit	$10.00	$10.00	$10.00	$10.00	$0.00	-$35.00		
29	Third Asset Profit	$4.00	$4.00	$4.00	$4.00	-$6.00	-$41.00		
30	Fourth Asset Profit	-$10.00	-$10.00	-$10.00	-$10.00	-$10.00	$25.00		
31	Total Profit	-$4.00	-$4.00	$6.00	$6.00	-$4.00	-$4.00		
32	Lowest Exer Price							-$40.00	$40.00
33	Med-Low Exer Price								
34	Med-High Exer Price								
35	Highest Exer Price								

How To Build This Spreadsheet Model.

1. Start with the Two Assets Spreadsheet. Open the spreadsheet that you created for Option Trading Strategies - Two Assets and immediately save the spreadsheet under a new name using the **File Save As** command.

2.Inputs for the Third and Fourth Assets. Create a place for the input information on the third and fourth assets. Copy the range **B5:B13** to the cell **B15**. For each asset, enter the new inputs (buy or sell, type, exercise price, and asset price) shown in Figure 1. Specifically, put the first asset inputs in the range **B5:B8**, second asset inputs in the range **B10:B13**, third asset inputs in the range **B15:B18**, and fourth asset inputs in the range **B20:B23**. Select the range **F2:H2**, click on **Edit Cut**, select the cell **B2**, and click on **Edit Paste**. To highlight the Third Asset, enter **=IF (B15=1,"Buy ","Sell ")&IF(B16=1,"Call",IF(B16=2,"Put","Stock"))** in cell **F2**. To highlight the Fourth Asset, enter **=IF(B20=1,"Buy ","Sell ")&IF(B21=1, "Call",IF(B21=2, "Put","Stock"))** in cell **H2**. Note that this spreadsheet uses the convention that the first asset in the one with the lowest exercise price, the second asset has the second lowest exercise price, the third has the third lowest exercise price, and the fourth asset has the highest exercise prices. Ties in exercise prices can be assigned either way.

3.Stock Price At Maturity. Make room and add the additional exercise price columns. Select the range **E26:I31**, click on **Edit Cut**, select the cell **G26**, and click on **Edit Paste**. Enter **=B7** in cell **C26**. Enter **=B12** in cell **D26**. Enter **=B17** in cell **E26**. Enter **=B22** in cell **F26**. Reference the third asset exercise price **=$E$26** in **L26** and copy the cell to the cell **M26**. Reference the fourth asset exercise price **=$F$26** in **N26** and copy the cell to the cell **O26**.

4.Asset Profits. Copy the range **B27:B28** to the range **C27:G27**. Insert two rows by selecting **A29:A30** and clicking on **Insert Rows**. The formulas for asset profits are:

- For a Call, the Profit = Max (Stock Price At Maturity - Exercise Price, 0) - Asset Price.

- For a Put, the Profit = Max (Exercise Price - Stock Price At Maturity, 0) - Asset Price.

- For a Stock, the Profit = Stock Price At Maturity - Asset Price

We need to multiply these profits by the Third Asset Buy or Sell switch in cell **B15** or by the corresponding Second Asset Buy or Sell switch in cell **B20**. For the Third Asset, Enter **=IF ($B$16=1,$B$15*(MAX(B$26-$B$17,0)-$B$18), IF($B$16=2,$B$15*(MAX($B$17-B$26,0) - $B$18), $B$15*(B$26-$B$18)))** in cell **B29** and copy this cell to the range **C29:G29**. For the Fourth Asset, Enter **=IF($B$21=1,$B$20*(MAX(B$26-$B$22,0)-$B$23), IF($B$21=2,$B$20* (MAX($B$22-B$26,0) -$B$23), $B$20*(B$26-$B$23)))** in cell **B30** and copy this cell to the range **C30:G30**.

5.Total Profit. The Total Profit = First Asset Profit + Second Asset Profit + Third Asset Profit + Fourth Asset Profit. Enter **=B27+B28+B29+B30** in cell **B31** and copy this cell to the range **C31:G31**.

6.Exercise Price Lines. When each asset is an option, add vertical lines on the graph for the third and fourth asset exercise prices. enter **-40** in cell **L34**, **=IF(B16=3,-40,40)** in cell **M34**, **-40** in cell **N35**, **=IF(B21=3,-40,40)** in cell **O35**.

7.Graph the Asset Profits and Exercise Prices. Click on the old graph and press the **Delete** key. Highlight the range **B26:O35**. Next choose **Insert Chart** from the main menu. Select an **XY (Scatter)** chart type and make other selections to complete the Chart Wizard. Place the graph in the range **C3:I25**.

FIGURE 2. Table of Option Trading Strategies

	J	K
1		
2	Low-High:	Buy Call, Sell Call
3		
4	No	Buying a Covered Call
5	No	Writing a Covered Call
6	No	Buying a Protective Put
7	No	Writing a Protective Put
8	Yes	Buying a Bullish Spread
9	No	Buying a Bearish Spread
10	No	Buying a Straddle
11	No	Writing a Straddle
12	No	Buying a Strangle
13	No	Writing a Strangle
14	No	Other Strategies

8.(Optional) Add An Option Trading Strategy Label. As a nice extra touch, add a label in cell **F1** which identifies the type of option trading strategy. Here are the steps to accomplish this:

- **Four asset label.** Combine the labels in **B2**, **D2**, **F2**, and **H2** (which are already in order from the lowest exercise price to the highest). Enter **=B2&", "&D2&", "&F2&", "&H2** in cell **K2**.

- **Buying a Butterfly Spread.** Test for Buy Call, Sell Call, Sell Call, Buy Call and the same second and third exercise price. Enter **=IF(AND(OR($K$2="Buy Call, Sell Call, Sell Call, Buy Call",$K$2="Buy Put, Sell Put, Sell Put, Buy Put"), $B$12=$B$17), "Yes","No")** in cell **J4**.

- **Writing a Butterfly Spread.** Test for Sell Call, Buy Call, Buy Call, Sell Call and the same second and third exercise price. Enter **=IF(AND(OR($K$2="Sell Call, Buy Call, Buy Call, Sell Call",$K$2="Sell Put, Buy Put, Buy Put, Sell Put"), $B$12=$B$17), "Yes","No")** in cell **J5**.

- **Other Strategies**. Test the range **J4:J5** for "Yes" cases. Enter **=IF (COUNTIF (J4:J5,"=Yes")>0,"No","Yes")** in cell **J6**.

- **Option Trading Strategy Label.** Determine which type of option trading strategy applies by looking for "Yes" in the range **J4:J6** using the **VLOOKUP** function. Enter **=VLOOKUP ("Yes",J4:K6,2,FALSE)** in cell **F1**.

Buying a butterfly spread is betting that there will be less volatility than the rest of the market thinks. Writing a butterfly spread is the opposite.

OPTION TRADING STRATEGIES
Problems

Problems To Build And Use The Spreadsheet Models

1.There are three types of trading strategies involving options: (1) strategies involving a single option and a stock, (2) spreads involving options of one type (i.e., two or more calls or two or more puts), and (3) combinations involving both call(s) and put(s). Build the **Option Trading Strategies - Two Assets** model and use it to graph all of the trading strategies involving two assets. In particular, show the following strategies:

(a.)First asset: Buy a stock for a stock price (asset price) of $41.25 and

Second asset: Sell a call with an exercise price of $47.39 for a call price of $5.83

= Buying a covered call.

(b.)First asset: Sell a stock for a stock price (asset price) of $36.47 and

Second asset: Buy a call with an exercise price of $32.83 for a call price of $6.74

= Writing a covered call.

(c.)First asset: Buy a stock for a stock price (asset price) of $43.72 and

Second asset: Buy a put with an exercise price of $47.87 for a put price of $7.31

= Buying a protective put.

(d.)First asset: Sell a stock for a stock price (asset price) of $36.93 and

Second asset: Sell a put with an exercise price of $33.29 for a put price of $6.36

= Writing a protective put.

(e.)First asset: Buy a call with an exercise price of $24.12 for a call price of $5.31 and

Second asset: Sell a call with an exercise price of $38.34 for a call price of $3.27

= Buying a bullish spread = Writing a bearish spread.

(f.)First asset: Sell a call with an exercise price of $18.92 for a call price of $7.39 and

Second asset: Buy a call with an exercise price of $45.72 with a call price of $3.78

= Buying a bearish spread = Writing a bullish spread.

(g.)<u>First asset:</u> Buy a call with an exercise price of $41.29 for a call price of $3.81 and

<u>Second asset:</u> Buy a put with an exercise price of $41.29 for a put price of $4.94

= Buying a straddle.

(h.)<u>First asset:</u> Sell a call with an exercise price of $38.47 for a call price of $2.93 and

<u>Second asset:</u> Sell a put with an exercise price of $38.47 for a put price of $5.63

= Writing a straddle.

(i.)<u>First asset:</u> Buy a call with an exercise price of $42.72 for a call price of $2.93 and

<u>Second asset:</u> Sell a put with an exercise price of $36.44 for a put price of $5.63

= Buying a strangle.

(j.)<u>First asset:</u> Buy a call with an exercise price of $46.18 for a call price ofÊ $3.58 and

<u>Second asset:</u> Sell a put with an exercise price of $38.50 for a put price of $6.39

= Writing a strangle.

2. Build the **Option Trading Strategies - Four Assets** model and use it to graph all of the trading strategies involving four assets. In particular, show:

(a.)<u>First asset:</u> Buy a call with an exercise price of $25.73 for a call price of $7.92 and

<u>Second asset:</u> Sell a call with an exercise price of $34.07 for a call price of $10.15

<u>Third asset:</u> Sell a call with an exercise price of $34.07 for a call price of $3.96 and

<u>Fourth asset:</u> Buy a call with an exercise price of $41.83 for a call price of $9.23

= Buying a butterfly spread using calls.

(b.)<u>First asset:</u> Buy a call with an exercise price of $23.84 for a call price of $5.39 and

<u>Second asset:</u> Sell a call with an exercise price of $36.19 for a call price of $6.98

<u>Third asset:</u> Sell a call with an exercise price of $36.19 for a call price of $3.36 and

<u>Fourth asset:</u> Buy a call with an exercise price of $47.28 for a call price of $8.34

= Writing a butterfly spread using calls.

(c.)<u>First asset:</u> Buy a put with an exercise price of $29.33 for a put price of $4.59 and

<u>Second asset:</u> Sell a put with an exercise price of $39.54 for a put price of $2.87

<u>Third asset:</u> Sell a put with an exercise price of $39.54 for a put price of $4.56 and

<u>Fourth asset:</u> Buy a put with an exercise price of $54.78 for a put price of $10.37

= Buying a butterfly spread using puts.

(d.)<u>First asset:</u> Buy a put with an exercise price of $27.49 for a put price of $3.22 and

<u>Second asset:</u> Sell a put with an exercise price of $41.38 for a put price of $5.39

<u>Third asset:</u> Sell a put with an exercise price of $41.38 for a put price of $2.74 and

<u>Fourth asset:</u> Buy a put with an exercise price of $52.86 for a put price of $9.49

= Writing a butterfly spread using puts.

PUT-CALL PARITY
Basics

Problem. Consider a call option and put option on the same underlying stock with the same exercise price and time to maturity. The call price is $4.00, the underlying stock price is $43.00, the exercise price on both options is $40.00, the riskfree rate is 5.00%, the time to maturity on both options is 0.25 years, and the stock pays a $2.00 / share dividend in 0.10 years. What is the price of the put price now?

FIGURE 1. Spreadsheet for Put-Call Parity - Basics.

	A	B	C
1	**PUT-CALL PARITY**	**Basics**	
2			
3	**Inputs**		
4	Call Price Now	$4.00	
5	Stock Price Now	$43.00	
6	Exercise Price	$40.00	
7	Riskfree Rate	5.00%	
8	Time To Maturity	0.25	
9	Dividend	$2.00	
10	Time To Dividend	0.10	
11			
12	**Outputs**		
13	Put Price Now	$2.51	

How To Build This Spreadsheet Model.

1.Inputs. Enter the inputs into the range **B4:B10**.

2.Put Price Now. The Put-Call Parity formula is Put Price Now = Call Price Now - Stock Price Now + Exercise Price / ((1 + Riskfree Rate)^(Time To Maturity)) + Dividend / ((1 + Riskfree Rate) ^(Time To Dividend)). Enter **=B4-B5+B6/((1+B7)^B8)+B9/((1+B7)^B10)** in cell **B13**.

Put-Call Parity predicts the Put Price is $2.51.

PUT-CALL PARITY
Payoff Diagram

The Put-Call Parity equation claims that one Put Option is equivalent to a replicating portfolio consisting of one Call Option, short one Stock, and a Bond paying a face value equal to the exercise price of the put and call options. Construct a payoff diagram to determine if the payoff at maturity of the replicating portfolio is equivalent to the payoff at maturity of a put option.

FIGURE 1. Spreadsheet for Put-Call Parity - Payoff Diagram.

	A	B	C	D	E	F	G	H	I
1	**PUT-CALL PARITY** Payoff Diagram								
2									
3	**Inputs**								
4	Call Price Now	$4.00							
5	Stock Price Now	$43.00							
6	Exercise Price	$40.00							
7	Riskfree Rate	5.00%							
8	Time To Maturity	0.25							
9	Dividend	$2.00							
10	Time To Dividend	0.10							
11									
12									
13									
14									
15									
16									
17									
18									
19	**Outputs**								
20	Stock Price at Maturity	$0.00	$8.00	$16.00	$24.00	$32.00	$40.00	$48.00	$56.00
21	Call Payoff	$0.00	$0.00	$0.00	$0.00	$0.00	$0.00	$8.00	$16.00
22	Short Stock Payoff	$0.00	-$8.00	-$16.00	-$24.00	-$32.00	-$40.00	-$48.00	-$56.00
23	Bond Payoff	$40.00	$40.00	$40.00	$40.00	$40.00	$40.00	$40.00	$40.00
24	Total Payoff	$40.00	$32.00	$24.00	$16.00	$8.00	$0.00	$0.00	$0.00
25	Exercise Price								
26									
27	Put Payoff	$40.00	$32.00	$24.00	$16.00	$8.00	$0.00	$0.00	$0.00

How To Build This Spreadsheet Model.

1.Start with the Basics Spreadsheet. Open the spreadsheet that you created for Put-Call Parity - Basics and immediately save the spreadsheet under a new name using the **File Save As** command.

2.Stock Price At Maturity. Enter **0, 8, 16, ..., 80** in the range **B20:L20**. Enter **=$B$6** in cell **M20** and copy the cell to cell **N20**.

3.Replicating Portfolio Payoff. Calculate the payoff on each piece of the replicating portfolio

- **Call Payoff** = Max(Stock Price At Maturity - Exercise Price, 0). Enter **=MAX(B20-$B$6,0)** in cell **B21** and copy the cell to the range **C21:L21**.

- **Short Stock Payoff** = -(Stock Price At Maturity). Enter **=-B20** in cell **B22** and copy the cell to the range **C22:L22**.

- **Bond Payoff** = Face Value = Exercise Price of the put and call options. Enter **=$B$6** in cell **B23** and copy the cell to the range **C23:L23**.

- **Total Payoff** = Sum of the Payoffs of the Three Replicating Portfolio Components. Enter **=SUM(B21:B23)** in cell **B24** and copy the cell to the range **C24:L24**.

4.Exercise Price. For convenience we wish to draw a vertical line at the exercise price by entering the upper and lower bound of the Y-axis. Enter **-80** in **M25** and **60** in **N25**.

5.Put Payoff. = Max(Exercise Price - Stock Price At Maturity, 0). Enter **=MAX($B$6-B20,0)** in cell **B27** and copy the cell to the range **C27:L27**.

6.Graph the Payoff on the Replicating Portfolio. Highlight the range **B20:N25**, click on **Insert Chart** from the main menu, and select an **XY(Scatter)** chart type and make other selections to complete the Chart Wizard. Place the graph in the range **C2:I19**.

Looking at the Total Payoff on the Replicating Portfolio (row **24**), we see that it matches the Put Payoff in row **27**. Looking at the Payoff Diagram we can see the payoff of each of the component of the replicating portfolio: (1) Call Payoff, (2) Short Stock Payoff, and (3) Bond Payoff. At each point on the X-axis, we vertically sum the three components to get the Total Payoff. The Payoff Diagram verifies that the Total Payoff has the same "hockey stick" payoff as a put option.

PUT-CALL PARITY
Problems

Problems To Build And Use The Spreadsheet Models

1. Consider a call option and put option on the same underlying stock with the same exercise price and time to maturity. The call price is $2.59, the underlying stock price is $28.63, the exercise price on both options is $26.18, the riskfree rate is 6.21%, the time to maturity on both options is 0.47 years, and the stock pays a $1.64 / share dividend in 0.28 years. Build the **Put-Call Parity - Basics** model and use it to determine the price of the put price now.

2. The Put-Call Parity equation claims that one Put Option is equivalent to a replicating portfolio consisting of one Call Option, short one Stock, and a Bond paying a face value equal to the exercise price of the put and call options. Build the **Put-Call Parity - Payoff Diagram** model and use it to determine if the payoff at maturity of the replicating portfolio is equivalent to the payoff at maturity of a put option.

BINOMIAL OPTION PRICING
Single Period

Problem. The current stock price of All-Net is $100.00, the potential up movement / period of All-Net's stock price is 30.00%, the potential down movement / period of All-Net's stock price is -20.00%, the risk-free rate is 2.0% per period, the exercise price of an one-period, European call option on All-Net is $90.00, the exercise price of an one-period, European put option on All-Net is $90.00, the time to maturity for both options is 0.75 years (nine months), and the number of periods for both options is 1. What are the current prices of the call and put?

Solution Strategy. First, calculate the date 1, maturity date items: stock up price, stock down price, and the corresponding call and put payoffs. Second, calculate the shares of stock and money borrowed to create a replicating portfolio that replicates the option payoff at maturity. Finally, calculate the price now of the replicating portfolio and, in the absence of arbitrage, this will be the option price now.

FIGURE 1. Spreadsheet Model of Binomial Option Pricing - Single Period - Call Option.

	A	B	C	D	E	F	G
1	**BINOMIAL OPTION PRICING**			Single Period			Call
2							
3	**Inputs**						
4	Option Type: 1=Call, 0=Put	1					
5	Stock Price Now	$100.00					
6	Up Movement / Period	30.00%					
7	Down Movement / Period	-20.00%					
8	Riskfree Rate / Period	2.00%					
9	Exercise Price	$90.00					
10	Time To Maturity (Years)	0.75					
11	Number of Periods	1					
12							
13		Now	Maturity				
14	Period	0	1				
15	Time	0.000	0.750				
16							
17	Stock	$100.00	$130.00				
18			$80.00				
19							
20	Call	$17.25	$40.00				
21			$0.00				
22							
23	**Replicating Portfolio**						
24							
25	**Stock Shares Bought (Sold)**						
26		0.800					
27							
28	**Money Lent (Borrowed)**						
29		($62.75)					

How To Build This Spreadsheet Model.

1. Inputs. Enter **1** in cell **B4** . This will serve as a switch between a call option and a put option. To highlight which type of option is being evaluated, enter **=IF($B$4=1,"Call","Put")** in cell **G1** and copy this cell to cell **A20**. Enter the other inputs into the range **B5:B11**.

2. Enter Periods and Time. Enter the periods **0** and **1** in cells **B14** and **C14**. The formula for Time = Time To Maturity * (Period / Number of Periods). Enter **=$B$10*(B14/$B$11)** in cell **B15** and copy the cell to cell **C15**.

3. Stock Prices. Set the Date 0 Stock Price equal to the Stock Price Now by entering **=B5** in cell **B17**. Calculate the Date 1 Stock Up Price = Stock Price Now * (1 + Up Movement / Period) by entering **=B17*(1+B6)** in cell **C17**. Calculate the Date 1 Stock Down Price = Stock Price Now * (1 + Down Movement / Period) by entering **=B17*(1+B7)** in cell **C18**.

4. Option Payoffs At Maturity. The formulas for option payoffs are:

- For a Call, the Payoff At Maturity = Max (Stock Price At Maturity - Exercise Price, 0).

- For a Put, the Payoff At Maturity = Max (Exercise Price - Stock Price At Maturity, 0).

- Enter **=IF($B$4=1,MAX(C17-$B$9,0),MAX($B$9-C17,0))** in cell **C20** and copy this cell to cell **C21**.

5. Create A Replicating Portfolio. For the Replicating Portfolio, calculate the Stock Shares Bought **(Sold)** using the Hedge Ratio = (Option Up Payoff - Option Down Payoff) / (Stock Up Price - Stock Down Price). In cell **B26**, enter **=(C20-C21)/(C17-C18)**. For the Replicating Portfolio, calculate the amount of Money Lent **(Borrowed)** = (Call Down Payoff -Hedge Ratio * Stock Down Price) / (1 + Riskfree Rate / Period). In cell **B29**, enter **=(C21-B26*C18)/(1+B8)**. Notice that replicating a Call option requires <u>Buying</u>Shares of Stock and <u>Borrowing</u> Money, whereas a Put option requires <u>Selling</u> Shares of Stock and <u>Lending</u> Money.

6. Calculate the Option Price Now. In the absence of arbitrage, the Option Price Now = Replicating Portfolio Price Now = Number of Shares of Stock * Stock Price Now + Money Borrowed. In cell **B20**, enter **=B26*B17+B29**.

We see that the Binomial Option Pricing model predicts a one-period European call price of $17.25. Now let's check the put.

FIGURE 2. Spreadsheet Model of Binomial Option Pricing - Single Period - Put Option.

	A	B	C	D	E	F	G
1	**BINOMIAL OPTION PRICING**			Single Period			Put
2							
3	**Inputs**						
4	Option Type: 1=Call, 0=Put	0					
5	Stock Price Now	$100.00					
6	Up Movement / Period	30.00%					
7	Down Movement / Period	-20.00%					
8	Riskfree Rate / Period	2.00%					
9	Exercise Price	$90.00					
10	Time To Maturity (Years)	0.75					
11	Number of Periods	1					
12							
13		Now	Maturity				
14	Period	0	1				
15	Time	0.000	0.750				
16							
17	Stock	$100.00	$130.00				
18			$80.00				
19							
20	Put	$5.49	$0.00				
21			$10.00				
22							
23	**Replicating Portfolio**						
24							
25	**Stock Shares Bought (Sold)**						
26		(0.200)					
27							
28	**Money Lent (Borrowed)**						
29		$25.49					

7. Put Option. Enter **0** in cell **B4**.

We see that the Binomial Option Pricing model predicts a one-period European put price of $5.49

BINOMIAL OPTION PRICING
Multi-Period

Problem. The current stock price of Energy Systems is $60.00, the potential up movement / period of Energy Systems' stock price is 10.00%, the potential down movement / period of Energy Systems' stock price is -5.00%, the risk-free rate is 0.5% per period, the exercise price of an one-period, European call option on Energy Systems is $65.00, the exercise price of an one-period, European put option on Energy Systems is $65.00, the time to maturity for both options is 2.00 years, and the number of periods for both options is 8. What are the current prices of the call and put?

Solution Strategy. First, build a multi-period tree of stock prices. Second, calculate call and put payoffs at maturity. Third, build the multi-period trees of the shares of stock and money borrowed to create a replicating portfolio that replicates the option period by period. Finally, build a multi-period tree of the value of the replicating portfolio and, in the absence of arbitrage, this will be value of the option.

FIGURE 1. Spreadsheet Model of Binomial Option Pricing - Multi-Period - Call Option.

		A	B	C	D	E	F	G	H	I	J
1		**BINOMIAL OPTION PRICING**			Multi-Period			Call			
2											
3		Inputs									
4		Option Type: 1=Call, 0=Put	1								
5		Stock Price Now	$60.00								
6		Up Movement / Period	10.00%								
7		Down Movement / Period	-5.00%								
8		Riskfree Rate / Period	0.50%								
9		Exercise Price	$65.00								
10		Time To Maturity (Years)	2.00								
11		Number of Periods	8								
12											
13			**Now**								**Maturity**
14		Period	0	1	2	3	4	5	6	7	8
15		Time	0.000	0.250	0.500	0.750	1.000	1.250	1.500	1.750	2.000
16											
17		**Stock**	$60.00	$66.00	$72.60	$79.86	$87.85	$96.63	$106.29	$116.92	$128.62
18				$57.00	$62.70	$68.97	$75.87	$83.45	$91.80	$100.98	$111.08
19					$54.15	$59.57	$65.52	$72.07	$79.28	$87.21	$95.93
20						$51.44	$56.59	$62.25	$68.47	$75.32	$82.85
21							$48.87	$53.76	$59.13	$65.05	$71.55
22								$46.43	$51.07	$56.18	$61.79
23									$44.11	$48.52	$53.37
24										$41.90	$46.09
25											$39.81
26											
27		**Call**	$3.93	$6.73	$10.94	$16.78	$24.13	$32.60	$41.94	$52.25	$63.62
28				$2.34	$4.34	$7.65	$12.66	$19.42	$27.44	$36.30	$46.08
29					$1.20	$2.46	$4.81	$8.84	$14.93	$22.53	$30.93
30						$0.48	$1.12	$2.52	$5.39	$10.64	$17.85
31							$0.12	$0.32	$0.87	$2.39	$6.55
32								$0.00	$0.00	$0.00	$0.00
33									$0.00	$0.00	$0.00
34										$0.00	$0.00
35											$0.00

How To Build This Spreadsheet Model.

1. Start with the Single Period Spreadsheet, Enter the Inputs, and Delete Rows. Open the spreadsheet that you created for Binomial Option Pricing - Single Period and immediately save the spreadsheet under a new name using the **File Save As** command. Enter the new inputs into the range **B5:B11**. Delete rows **20** through **29** by selecting the range **A20:A29**, clicking on **Edit**, **Delete**, selecting the **Entire Row** radio button on the **Delete** dialog box, and clicking on **OK**.

2. Enter Periods and Time. Enter the periods **0, 1, 2, ..., 8** in cells **B14** and **J14**. The formula for Time = Time To Maturity * (Period / Number of Periods). Enter **=$B$10*(B14/$B$11)** in cell **B15** and copy the cell to the range **C15:J15**.

3. The Stock Price Tree. As in the single period case, the Period 0 Stock Price is equal to the Stock Price Now. Turning to the rest of the Stock Price Tree, we want to create the entire tree with one copy command to a square range. To do this we have to determine whether a cell in the square area is on the tree or off the tree. Further, there are two different formulas to use on the tree (a Down Price vs. an Up Price). Hence, there are three possibilities:

- When the cell to the left and the cell diagonally to the upper left are both blank, then show a blank.

- When the cell to the left is blank and the cell diagonally to the upper left has a number, then you are on the lower edge of the triangle so calculate the Down Price = (Stock Price in the Upper Left) * (1 + Down Movement / Period).

- When both cells have numbers, then calculate the Up Price = (Stock Price to the Left) * (1 + Up Movement / Period)

Enter **=IF(B17="",IF(B16="","",B16*(1+$B$7)), B17*(1+$B$6))** in cell **C17** and copy this cell to the 9-by-9 square range **C17:J25**. The nested IF statements cause a binomial tree to form in the triangular area from **C17** to **J17** to **J25**. Incidentally, the same procedure could create a binomial tree for any number of periods. For example, if you wished to create a 20 period model, then you would simply copy this cell to a 20-by-21 square range. In the **Binomial Option Pricing: Full-Scale Real Data** spreadsheet model, we will exploit this feature to create a 50 period model!

4. Option Payoffs At Maturity. Copy the option type indicator from cell **G1** and copy this cell to cell **A27**. The formulas for option payoffs are:

- For a Call, the Payoff At Maturity = Max (Stock Price At Maturity - Exercise Price, 0).

- For a Put, the Payoff At Maturity = Max (Exercise Price - Stock Price Maturity, 0).

Enter **=IF($B$4=1,MAX(J17-$B$9,0),MAX($B$9-J17,0))** in cell **J27** and copy this cell to the range **J28:J35**.

FIGURE 2. Spreadsheet Model of Binomial Option Pricing - Multi-Period - Call Option (Continued).

		A	B	C	D	E	F	G	H	I	J
1		**BINOMIAL OPTION PRICING**			Multi-Period			Call			
2											
3		Inputs									
4		Option Type: 1=Call, 0=Put	1								
5		Stock Price Now	$60.00								
6		Up Movement / Period	10.00%								
7		Down Movement / Period	-5.00%								
8		Riskfree Rate / Period	0.50%								
9		Exercise Price	$65.00								
10		Time To Maturity (Years)	2.00								
11		Number of Periods	8								
12											
13			Now								Maturity
14		Period	0	1	2	3	4	5	6	7	8
15		Time	0.000	0.250	0.500	0.750	1.000	1.250	1.500	1.750	2.000
37		Replicating Portfolio									
38											
39		Stock Shares Bought (Sold)									
40			0.487	0.667	0.838	0.958	1.000	1.000	1.000	1.000	
41				0.367	0.552	0.758	0.929	1.000	1.000	1.000	
42					0.244	0.413	0.644	0.882	1.000	1.000	
43						0.130	0.259	0.484	0.803	1.000	
44							0.043	0.108	0.269	0.671	
45								0.000	0.000	0.000	
46									0.000	0.000	
47										0.000	
48											
49		Money Lent (Borrowed)									
50				($25.32)	($37.28)	($49.93)	($59.71)	($63.72)	($64.03)	($64.35)	($64.68)
51					($18.60)	($30.26)	($44.66)	($57.86)	($64.03)	($64.35)	($64.68)
52						($11.99)	($22.16)	($37.36)	($54.74)	($64.35)	($64.68)
53							($6.20)	($13.53)	($27.59)	($49.61)	($64.68)
54								($2.00)	($5.50)	($15.06)	($41.28)
55									$0.00	$0.00	$0.00
56										$0.00	$0.00
57											$0.00

5. The Stock Shares Bought (Sold) Tree. At each point in the 8-by-8 square range, you need to determine if you are on the tree or off the tree. There are two possibilities:

- When the corresponding cell in the Stock Price area is blank, then show a blank.

- When the corresponding cell in the Stock Price area has a number, then use the Hedge Ratio = (Option Up Payoff - Option Down Payoff) / (Stock Up Price - Stock Down Price).

Enter **=IF(C28="","",(C27-C28)/(C17-C18))** in cell **B40** and copy this cell to the 8-by-8 square range **B40:I47**. A binomial tree will form in the triangular area from **B40** to **I40** to **I47**. Again the same procedure could create a binominal tree for any number of periods.

6. The Money Lent (Borrowed) Tree. At each point in the 8-by-8 square range, you need to determine if you are on the tree or off the tree. There are two possibilities:

- When the corresponding cell in the Stock Price area is blank, then show a blank.

- When the corresponding cell in the Stock Price area has a number, then calculate the amount of Money Lent **(Borrowed)** = (Call Down Payoff ÐHedge Ratio * Stock Down Price) / (1 + Riskfree Rate / Period).

Enter **=IF(C28="","",(C28-B40*C18)/(1+$B$8))** in cell **B50** and copy this cell to the 8-by-8 square range **B50:I57**. A binomial tree will form in the triangular area from **B50** to **I50** to **I57**. Again the same procedure could create a binominal tree for any number of periods.

7.The Option Price Tree. At each point in the 8-by-8 square range (excluding column **J** containing option payoffs at maturity), you need to determine if you are on the tree or off the tree. There are two possibilities:

- When the corresponding cell in the Stock Price area is blank, then show a blank.

- When the corresponding cell in the Stock Price area has a number, then (in the absence of arbitrage) the Option Price At Each Node = Price Of The Corresponding Replicating Portfolio = Number of Shares of Stock * Stock Price + Money Borrowed.

Enter **=IF(C28="","",B40*B17+B50)** in cell **B27** and copy this cell to the 8-by-9 range **B27:I34**. **Be sure not to copy over column J containing option payoffs at maturity**. A binomial tree will form in the triangular area from **B27** to **J27** to **J35**. Again the same procedure could create a binominal tree for any number of periods. We see that the Binomial Option Pricing model predicts an eight-period European call price of $3.93. Now let's check the put.

FIGURE 3. Spreadsheet Model of Binomial Option Pricing - Multi-Period - Put Option.

	A	B	C	D	E	F	G	H	I	J
1	**BINOMIAL OPTION PRICING** Multi-Period						**Put**			
2										
3	**Inputs**									
4	Option Type: 1=Call, 0=Put	0								
5	Stock Price Now	$60.00								
6	Up Movement / Period	10.00%								
7	Down Movement / Period	-5.00%								
8	Riskfree Rate / Period	0.50%								
9	Exercise Price	$65.00								
10	Time To Maturity (Years)	2.00								
11	Number of Periods	8								
12										
13		**Now**								**Maturity**
14	**Period**	0	1	2	3	4	5	6	7	8
15	**Time**	0.000	0.250	0.500	0.750	1.000	1.250	1.500	1.750	2.000
16										
17	**Stock**	$60.00	$66.00	$72.60	$79.86	$87.85	$96.63	$106.29	$116.92	$128.62
18			$57.00	$62.70	$68.97	$75.87	$83.45	$91.80	$100.98	$111.08
19				$54.15	$59.57	$65.52	$72.07	$79.28	$87.21	$95.93
20					$51.44	$56.59	$62.25	$68.47	$75.32	$82.85
21						$48.87	$53.76	$59.13	$65.05	$71.55
22							$46.43	$51.07	$56.18	$61.79
23								$44.11	$48.52	$53.37
24									$41.90	$46.09
25										$39.81
26										
27	**Put**	$6.39	$3.50	$1.43	$0.32	$0.00	$0.00	$0.00	$0.00	$0.00
28			$8.11	$4.72	$2.08	$0.51	$0.00	$0.00	$0.00	$0.00
29				$10.13	$6.29	$3.01	$0.80	$0.00	$0.00	$0.00
30					$12.44	$8.25	$4.30	$1.27	$0.00	$0.00
31						$14.96	$10.60	$6.09	$2.02	$0.00
32							$17.61	$13.29	$8.50	$3.21
33								$20.25	$16.16	$11.63
34									$22.78	$18.91
35										$25.19

8.Put Option. Enter **0** in cell **B4**.

We see that the Binomial Option Pricing model predicts an eight-period European put price of $6.39.

FIGURE 4. Spreadsheet Model of Binomial Option Pricing - Multi-Period - Put Option (Continued).

	A	B	C	D	E	F	G	H	I	J
1	**BINOMIAL OPTION PRICING**			**Multi-Period**			**Put**			
2										
3	**Inputs**									
4	Option Type: 1=Call, 0=Put	0								
5	Stock Price Now	$60.00								
6	Up Movement / Period	10.00%								
7	Down Movement / Period	-5.00%								
8	Riskfree Rate / Period	0.50%								
9	Exercise Price	$65.00								
10	Time To Maturity (Years)	2.00								
11	Number of Periods	8								
12										
13		**Now**								**Maturity**
14	**Period**	**0**	**1**	**2**	**3**	**4**	**5**	**6**	**7**	**8**
15	**Time**	**0.000**	**0.250**	**0.500**	**0.750**	**1.000**	**1.250**	**1.500**	**1.750**	**2.000**
37	**Replicating Portfolio**									
38										
39	**Stock Shares Bought (Sold)**									
40		(0.513)	(0.333)	(0.162)	(0.042)	0.000	0.000	0.000	0.000	
41			(0.633)	(0.448)	(0.242)	(0.071)	0.000	0.000	0.000	
42				(0.756)	(0.587)	(0.356)	(0.118)	0.000	0.000	
43					(0.870)	(0.741)	(0.516)	(0.197)	0.000	
44						(0.957)	(0.892)	(0.731)	(0.329)	
45							(1.000)	(1.000)	(1.000)	
46								(1.000)	(1.000)	
47									(1.000)	
48										
49	**Money Lent (Borrowed)**									
50		$37.14	$25.49	$13.16	$3.69	$0.00	$0.00	$0.00	$0.00	
51			$44.17	$32.83	$18.74	$5.85	$0.00	$0.00	$0.00	
52				$51.09	$41.24	$26.35	$9.29	$0.00	$0.00	
53					$57.20	$50.19	$36.44	$14.74	$0.00	
54						$61.71	$58.54	$49.29	$23.39	
55							$64.03	$64.35	$64.68	
56								$64.35	$64.68	
57									$64.68	

As in the single period case, replicating a Call option requires **Buying** Shares of Stock and **Borrowing** Money, whereas a Put option requires **Selling** Shares of Stock and **Lending** Money. Notice that the quantity of Money Borrowed or Lent and the quantity of Shares Bought or Sold changes over time and differs for up nodes vs. down nodes. This process of changing the replicating portfolio every period based on the realized up or down movement in the underlying stock price is called dynamic replication.

Price accuracy can be increased by subdividing the interval into more periods (15, 30, etc.). Typically, from 30 subperiods to 100 periods are required in order to achieve price accuracy to the penny.

BINOMIAL OPTION PRICING
Risk Neutral

The previous spreadsheet model, **Binomial Option Pricing: Multi-Period**, determined the price of an option by constructing a replicating portfolio, which combines a stock and a bond to replicate the payoffs of the option. An alternative way to price an option is the Risk Neutral method. Both techniques give you the same answer. The main advantage of the Risk Neutral method is that it is faster and easier to implement. The Replicating Portfolio method required the construction of four trees (stock prices, shares of stock **bought (sold)**, money **lent (borrowed)**, and option prices). The Risk Neutral method will only require two trees (stock prices and option prices).

FIGURE 1. Spreadsheet Model of Binomial Option Pricing - Risk Neutral - Call Option.

		A	B	C	D	E	F	G	H	I	J
1		**BINOMIAL OPTION PRICING**			**Risk Neutral**			**Call**			
2											
3		**Inputs**				**Outputs**					
4		Option Type: 1=Call, 0=Put	1		Risk Neutral Probability		36.67%				
5		Stock Price Now	$60.00								
6		Up Movement / Period	10.00%								
7		Down Movement / Period	-5.00%								
8		Riskfree Rate / Period	0.50%								
9		Exercise Price	$65.00								
10		Time To Maturity (Years)	2.00								
11		Number of Periods	8								
12											
13			**Now**								**Maturity**
14		**Period**	0	1	2	3	4	5	6	7	8
15		**Time**	0.000	0.250	0.500	0.750	1.000	1.250	1.500	1.750	2.000
16											
17		**Stock**	$60.00	$66.00	$72.60	$79.86	$87.85	$96.63	$106.29	$116.92	$128.62
18				$57.00	$62.70	$68.97	$75.87	$83.45	$91.80	$100.98	$111.08
19					$54.15	$59.57	$65.52	$72.07	$79.28	$87.21	$95.93
20						$51.44	$56.59	$62.25	$68.47	$75.32	$82.85
21							$48.87	$53.76	$59.13	$65.05	$71.55
22								$46.43	$51.07	$56.18	$61.79
23									$44.11	$48.52	$53.37
24										$41.90	$46.09
25											$39.81
26											
27		**Call**	$3.93	$6.73	$10.94	$16.78	$24.13	$32.60	$41.94	$52.25	$63.62
28				$2.34	$4.34	$7.65	$12.66	$19.42	$27.44	$36.30	$46.08
29					$1.20	$2.46	$4.81	$8.84	$14.93	$22.53	$30.93
30						$0.48	$1.12	$2.52	$5.39	$10.64	$17.85
31							$0.12	$0.32	$0.87	$2.39	$6.55
32								$0.00	$0.00	$0.00	$0.00
33									$0.00	$0.00	$0.00
34										$0.00	$0.00
35											$0.00

How To Build This Spreadsheet Model.

1.Start with the Multi-Period Spreadsheet. Open the spreadsheet that you created for Binomial Option Pricing - Multi-Period and immediately save the spreadsheet under a new name using the **File Save As** command.

2.Risk Neutral Probability. Calculate the Risk Neutral Probability = (Riskfree Rate / Period - Down Movement / Period) / (Up Movement / Period - Down Movement / Period). Enter **=(B8-B7)/ (B6-B7)** in cell **F4**.

FIGURE 2. Spreadsheet Model of Binomial Option Pricing - Risk Neutral - Put Option.

	A	B	C	D	E	F	G	H	I	J
1	**BINOMIAL OPTION PRICING**			Risk Neutral			Put			
2										
3	**Inputs**				Outputs					
4	Option Type: 1=Call, 0=Put	0		Risk Neutral Probability		36.67%				
5	Stock Price Now	$60.00								
6	Up Movement / Period	10.00%								
7	Down Movement / Period	-5.00%								
8	Riskfree Rate / Period	0.50%								
9	Exercise Price	$65.00								
10	Time To Maturity (Years)	2.00								
11	Number of Periods	8								
12										
13		Now								Maturity
14	Period	0	1	2	3	4	5	6	7	8
15	Time	0.000	0.250	0.500	0.750	1.000	1.250	1.500	1.750	2.000
16										
17	Stock	$60.00	$66.00	$72.60	$79.86	$87.85	$96.63	$106.29	$116.92	$128.62
18			$57.00	$62.70	$68.97	$75.87	$83.45	$91.80	$100.98	$111.08
19				$54.15	$59.57	$65.52	$72.07	$79.28	$87.21	$95.93
20					$51.44	$56.59	$62.25	$68.47	$75.32	$82.85
21						$48.87	$53.76	$59.13	$65.05	$71.55
22							$46.43	$51.07	$56.18	$61.79
23								$44.11	$48.52	$53.37
24									$41.90	$46.09
25										$39.81
26										
27	Put	$6.39	$3.50	$1.43	$0.32	$0.00	$0.00	$0.00	$0.00	$0.00
28			$8.11	$4.72	$2.08	$0.51	$0.00	$0.00	$0.00	$0.00
29				$10.13	$6.29	$3.01	$0.80	$0.00	$0.00	$0.00
30					$12.44	$8.25	$4.30	$1.27	$0.00	$0.00
31						$14.96	$10.60	$6.09	$2.02	$0.00
32							$17.61	$13.29	$8.50	$3.21
33								$20.25	$16.16	$11.63
34									$22.78	$18.91
35										$25.19

3.The Option Price Tree. At each point in the 8-by-9 range, you need to determine if you are on the tree or off the tree. There are two possibilities:

- When the corresponding cell in the Stock Price area is blank, then show a blank.

- When the corresponding cell in the Stock Price area has a number, then (in the absence of arbitrage) the Option Price At Each Node = Expected Value of the Option Price Next Period (using the Risk Neutral Probability) Discounted At The Riskfree Rate = [(Risk Neutral Probability) * (Stock Up Price) + (1 - Risk Neutral Probability) * (Stock Down Price)] / (1+ Riskfree Rate / Period).

Enter **=IF(C28="","",($F$4*C27+(1-$F$4)*C28)/(1+$B$8))** in cell **B27** (yielding a blank output at first) and then copy this cell to the 8-by-8 range **B27:I34**. **Be sure not to copy over column J containing option payoffs at maturity.** A binomial tree will form in the triangular area from **B27** to **J27** to **J35**. Again the same procedure could create a binominal tree for any number of periods. For appearances, delete rows **37** through **57** by selecting the range **A37:A57**, clicking on **Edit**, **Delete**, selecting the **Entire Row** radio button on the **Delete** dialog box, and clicking on **OK**.

We see that the Risk Neutral method predicts an eight-period European call price of $3.93. This is identical to Replicating Portfolio Price. Now let's check the put.

4.Put Option. Enter **0** in cell **B4**.

We see that the Risk Neutral method predicts an eight-period European put price of $6.39. This is identical to Replicating Portfolio Price. Again, we get the same answer either way. The advantage of the Risk Neutral method is that we only have to construct two trees, rather than four trees.

BINOMIAL OPTION PRICING
Full-Scale Real Data

The binomial model can be used to price real-world European calls and puts. Further, the Binomial Tree / Risk Neutral method can be extended to price *any* type of derivative security (European vs. American vs. other, on any underlying asset(s), with any underlying dividends or cash flows, with any derivative payoffs at maturity and/or payoffs before maturity). Indeed, it is one of the most popular techniques on Wall Street for pricing and hedging derivatives.

Problem Using Real Data. On December 13, 1999, the stock price of Amazon.com was $102.50, the yield on a risk-free Treasury Bill maturing on April 20, 2000 was 5.47%, the exercise price of an April 100 European call on Amazon.com was $100.00, the exercise price of an April 100 European put on Amazon.com was $100.00, and the time to maturity for both April 21, 2000 maturity options was 0.3556 years. What is the annual standard deviation of Amazon.com stock? What are the current prices of the call and put under the *continuous* annualization convention? What are the current prices of the call and put under the *discrete* annualization convention?

Solution Strategy. Collect Amazon.com's historical stock prices from Yahoo Finance! and calculate the annual standard deviation. Use the annual standard deviation and the annual riskfree rate to calculate the up movement / period, down movement / period, and riskfree rate / period. Extend the Binomial Option Pricing - Risk Neutral model to full-scale (50 periods) in order to achieve greater price accuracy.

FIGURE 1. Spreadsheet Model of Binomial Option Pricing - Estimating Volatility.

	A	B	C	D	E	F	G	H
1	**BINOMIAL OPTION PRICING**					**Estimating Volatility**		
2								
3	Date	Open	High	Low	Close	Volume	Discrete Return	Continuous Return
4	13-Dec-99	106.6250	106.6250	101.5000	102.5000	8,653,700	-3.93%	-4.00%
5	10-Dec-99	111.9375	112.0000	104.4375	106.6875	14,929,000	2.96%	2.91%
6	9-Dec-99	95.5000	113.0000	93.4375	103.6250	41,364,600	17.01%	15.71%
7	8-Dec-99	86.8125	93.0000	86.0000	88.5625	12,867,200	2.90%	2.86%
8	7-Dec-99	88.0000	88.0000	84.3750	86.0625	6,727,100	-1.92%	-1.94%
9	6-Dec-99	86.8750	89.8750	84.6875	87.7500	9,199,200	1.37%	1.36%
10	3-Dec-99	92.5000	93.3750	86.0625	86.5625	11,151,200	-2.81%	-2.85%
11	2-Dec-99	86.0000	91.3125	85.6250	89.0625	9,538,700	4.78%	4.67%
12	1-Dec-99	87.2500	87.8750	81.9688	85.0000	10,663,600	-0.07%	-0.07%
13	30-Nov-99	88.2656	88.8750	83.8125	85.0625	13,465,500	-5.94%	-6.13%
14	29-Nov-99	95.5000	96.8750	90.1250	90.4375	18,053,700	-2.89%	-2.93%
62	22-Sep-99	62.8750	66.5000	60.6875	66.0000	10,037,500	6.02%	5.85%
63	21-Sep-99	61.6250	63.9375	61.0000	62.2500	8,232,500	-0.80%	-0.80%
64	20-Sep-99	63.6875	65.0000	62.6875	62.7500	5,957,100	-1.67%	-1.68%
65	17-Sep-99	65.6250	66.0000	62.7500	63.8125	7,239,500	-2.20%	-2.23%
66	16-Sep-99	64.9375	65.8125	62.7500	65.2500	7,058,900	-0.48%	-0.48%
67	15-Sep-99	67.7500	67.9375	65.0000	65.5625	7,817,300	-0.66%	-0.67%
68	14-Sep-99	62.7500	66.4375	62.7500	66.0000	8,782,800	4.24%	4.16%
69	13-Sep-99	65.6250	66.0000	62.5000	63.3125	7,747,600		
70								
71					Standard Deviation (Daily)		5.68%	5.42%
72					Standard Deviation (Annual)		90.23%	86.07%

How To Build This Spreadsheet Model.

1.Collect Historical Stock Price Data. Go to <u>Yahoo Finance!</u> (<u>quote.yahoo.com</u>), enter **AMZN** (the ticker symbol for Amazon.com) in the **Get Quotes** box, click on **Chart**, at the bottom of the page click on **Table: daily**, adjust the start date if you want more than three months of data, click on **Download Spreadsheet Format**, and save the **csv** file. Launch Excel and open the **csv** file.

2.Calculate Discrete and Continuous Returns. There are two conventions for calculating stock returns. A simple percent change yields the Discrete Return = [(Price on date t) - (Price on date t-1)] / (Price on date t-1). Enter **=(E4-E5)/E5** in cell **G4** and copy this cell to the range **G5:G68**. The Continuous Return = LN[(Price on date t) / (Price on date t-1)]. Enter **=LN(E4/E5)** in cell **H4** and copy this cell to the range **H5:H68**.

FIGURE 2. Spreadsheet Model of Binomial Option Pricing - Full-Scale Real Data - Call Option.

	A	B	C	D	E	F	AX	AY	AZ
1	**BINOMIAL OPTION PRICING**			**Full-Scale Real Data**					
2				Call	Continuous				
3	**Inputs**				Outputs				
4	Option Type: 1=Call, 0=Put	1		Time / Period		0.007			
5	Stock Price Now	$102.50		Riskfree Rate / Period		0.04%			
6	Standard Dev (Annual)	86.07%		Up Movement / Period		7.53%			
7	Riskfree Rate (Annual)	5.47%		Down Movement / Period		-7.00%			
8	Exercise Price	$100.00		Risk Neutral Probability		48.45%			
9	Time To Maturity (Years)	0.3556							
10	Number of Periods	50							
11	Annualization Convention: 1=Discrete, 0=Continuous	0							
12									
13		**Now**							**Maturity**
14	Period	**0**	**1**	**2**	**3**	**4**	**48**	**49**	**50**
15	Time	**0.000**	**0.007**	**0.014**	**0.021**	**0.028**	**0.341**	**0.348**	**0.356**
16									
17	Stock	$102.50	$110.22	$118.51	$127.44	$137.03	$3,340.75	$3,592.25	$3,862.69
18			$95.32	$102.50	$110.22	$118.51	$2,889.33	$3,106.85	$3,340.75
19				$88.65	$95.32	$102.50	$2,498.91	$2,687.04	$2,889.33
20					$82.44	$88.65	$2,161.24	$2,323.95	$2,498.91
21						$76.67	$1,869.20	$2,009.93	$2,161.24
22							$1,616.63	$1,738.33	$1,869.20
23							$1,398.18	$1,503.44	$1,616.63
24							$1,209.25	$1,300.29	$1,398.18
25							$1,045.85	$1,124.59	$1,209.25
26							$904.53	$972.63	$1,045.85
27							$782.31	$841.20	$904.53
28							$676.60	$727.53	$782.31
29							$585.17	$629.23	$676.60
30							$506.10	$544.20	$585.17
31							$437.71	$470.67	$506.10
32							$378.57	$407.07	$437.71
33							$327.41	$352.06	$378.57
34							$283.17	$304.49	$327.41
35							$244.91	$263.35	$283.17
36							$211.82	$227.76	$244.91

3.Calculate the Daily and Annual Standard Deviation. Use Excel's function **STDEV** to calculate the sample standard deviation of daily discrete returns and daily continuous returns. Enter **=STDEV(G4:G68)** in cell **G71** and copy the cell to **H71**. Convert the daily standard deviation to annual standard deviation by multiplying by the square root of the number of trading days in the year. By way of explanation, the stock variance is proportion to the units of time. Hence, the stock standard deviation is proportional to the square root of the units of time. The empirical evidence shows that is better to use trading days rather than calendar days, since trading days is a better predictor of stock volatility than calendar days. There are 252 trading days in the year, so we multiply by the square root of 252. Enter **=G71*SQRT(252)** in cell **G72** and copy the cell to **H72**.

We find that Amazon.com's annual standard deviation is 90.23% based on discrete returns and is 86.07% based on continuous returns.

4.Start with the Risk Neutral Spreadsheet and Freeze Panes. Open the spreadsheet that you created for Binomial Option Pricing - Risk Neutral and immediately save the spreadsheet under a new name using the **File Save As** command. It will be helpful for navigation purposes to lock in both column titles and row titles. Select cell **G16** and click on **Window Freeze Panes**.

5.Rearrange the Inputs. Select the range **A6:B7** and drag the range (hover the cursor over the lower highlighted line, click on the left mouse button, and hold it down while you move it) to cell **E6**. Select the range **A8:B8** and drag the range to cell **E5**. Select the range **A9:B11** and drag the range to cell **A8**. Select the range **E4:F4** and drag the range to cell **E8**.

6.Enter the New Inputs. Enter the Full-Scale Real Data inputs in the range **B4:B11** as shown in **Figure 2**. The value in cell **B11** serves as a switch between the Discrete and Continuous Annualization Conventions. To accommodate both annualization conventions, enter **=IF (B11=1,90.23%,86.07%)** in cell **B6** for the Annual Standard Deviation. To highlight which annualization convention is in use, enter **=IF($B$11=1,"Discrete","Continuous")** in cell **E2**.

7.Calculate the New Outputs. Calculate four new "per period" outputs:

- **Time / Period** = (Time To Maturity) / (Number of Periods). Enter **=B9/B10** in cell **F4**.

- **Riskfree Rate / Period** = (Annual Riskfree Rate) * (Time / Period) under the discrete annualization convention or = exp[(Annual Riskfree Rate) * (Time / Period)] -1 under the continuous annualization convention. Enter **=IF($B$11=1,B7*F4,EXP(B7*F4)-1)** in cell **F5**.

- **Up Movement / Period** = (Annual Standard Deviation) * Square Root (Time / Period) under the discrete annualization convention or = exp[(Annual Standard Deviation) * Square Root (Time / Period)] -1 under the continuous annualization convention. Enter **=IF ($B$11=1,B6*SQRT(F4),EXP(B6*SQRT(F4))-1)** in cell **F6**.

- **Down Movement / Period** = -(Annual Standard Deviation) * Square Root (Time / Period) under the discrete annualization convention or = exp[-(Annual Standard Deviation) * Square Root (Time / Period)] -1 under the continuous annualization convention. Enter **=IF**

($B$11=1,-B6*SQRT(F4),EXP(-B6*SQRT(F4))-1) in cell **F7**.

The up movement / period and down movement / period are calibrated to correspond to the stock's annual standard deviation. It is not necessary to calibrate them to the stock's expected return.[1]

8.Extend The Periods and Time to 50 Periods. Select the range **B14:C14**, grab the fill bar (hover the mouse over the lower-right corner of the selection - when it turns to a "+" sign, click the left mouse button), and fill in the range **D14:AZ14**. Select the cell **B15** and copy it to the range **C15:AZ15**.

9.Extend The Stock Price Tree to 50 Periods. Add some rows to make space between the Stock Price Tree and the Option Price Tree. Select the range **A26:A67** and click on **Insert Rows**. Then, copy cell **C17** to the 50-by-51 range **C17:AZ67**. A binomial tree will form in the triangular area from **C17** to **AZ17** to **AZ67**.

FIGURE 3. Spreadsheet Model of Binomial Option Pricing - Full-Scale Real Data - Call Option (Continued).

	A	B	C	D	E	F	AX	AY	AZ
1	**BINOMIAL OPTION PRICING**			**Full-Scale Real Data**					
2				Call	Continuous				
3	Inputs				Outputs				
4	Option Type: 1=Call, 0=Put	1		Time / Period		0.007			
5	Stock Price Now	$102.50		Riskfree Rate / Period		0.04%			
6	Standard Dev (Annual)	86.07%		Up Movement / Period		7.53%			
7	Riskfree Rate (Annual)	5.47%		Down Movement / Period		-7.00%			
8	Exercise Price	$100.00		Risk Neutral Probability		48.45%			
9	Time To Maturity (Years)	0.3556							
10	Number of Periods	50							
11	Annualization Convention: 1=Discrete, 0=Continuous	0							
12									
13			Now						Maturity
14		Period	0	1	2	3	4	48	49	50
15		Time	0.000	0.007	0.014	0.021	0.028	0.341	0.348	0.356
68										
69		Call	$22.61	$27.48	$33.15	$39.68	$47.15	$3,240.82	$3,492.29	$3,762.69
70				$18.04	$22.17	$27.04	$32.70	$2,789.40	$3,006.89	$3,240.75
71					$14.17	$17.62	$21.73	$2,398.98	$2,587.07	$2,789.33
72						$10.94	$13.77	$2,061.32	$2,223.99	$2,398.91
73							$8.28	$1,769.28	$1,909.97	$2,061.24
74								$1,516.71	$1,638.37	$1,769.20
75								$1,298.26	$1,403.48	$1,516.63
76								$1,109.33	$1,200.33	$1,298.18
77								$945.93	$1,024.63	$1,109.25
78								$804.61	$872.67	$945.85
79								$682.38	$741.24	$804.53
80								$576.68	$627.57	$682.31
81								$485.25	$529.27	$576.60
82								$406.18	$444.24	$485.17
83								$337.79	$370.71	$406.10
84								$278.65	$307.11	$337.71
85								$227.49	$252.10	$278.57
86								$183.25	$204.53	$227.41
87								$144.99	$163.39	$183.17
88								$111.89	$127.80	$144.91

10. Extend The Option Payoffs At Maturity to 50 Periods. Copy the old payoffs at maturity starting in cell **J69** and to the new payoffs at maturity range **AZ69:AZ119**.

11. Extend The Option Price Tree to 50 Periods. Copy cell **B69** to the range **B69:AY118**. A binomial tree will form in the triangular area from **B69** to **AZ69** to **AZ119**.

We see that the Full-Scale Real Data model predicts an European call price of $22.61. This is only one cent different that what the Black-Scholes model predicts given identical inputs! Now let's check the put.

FIGURE 4. Spreadsheet Model of Binomial Option Pricing - Full-Scale Real Data - Put Option.

	A	B	C	D	E	F	AX	AY	AZ
1	**BINOMIAL OPTION PRICING**			**Full-Scale Real Data**					
2				Put	Continuous				
3	Inputs				Outputs				
4	Option Type: 1=Call, 0=Put	0		Time / Period		0.007			
5	Stock Price Now	$102.50		Riskfree Rate / Period		0.04%			
6	Standard Dev (Annual)	86.07%		Up Movement / Period		7.53%			
7	Riskfree Rate (Annual)	5.47%		Down Movement / Period		-7.00%			
8	Exercise Price	$100.00		Risk Neutral Probability		48.45%			
9	Time To Maturity (Years)	0.3556							
10	Number of Periods	50							
11	Annualization Convention: 1=Discrete, 0=Continuous	0							
12									
13		**Now**							**Maturity**
14	**Period**	**0**	**1**	**2**	**3**	**4**	**48**	**49**	**50**
15	**Time**	**0.000**	**0.007**	**0.014**	**0.021**	**0.028**	**0.341**	**0.348**	**0.356**
16									
17	**Stock**	$102.50	$110.22	$118.51	$127.44	$137.03	$3,340.75	$3,592.25	$3,862.69
18			$95.32	$102.50	$110.22	$118.51	$2,889.33	$3,106.85	$3,340.75
19				$88.65	$95.32	$102.50	$2,498.91	$2,687.04	$2,889.33
20					$82.44	$88.65	$2,161.24	$2,323.95	$2,498.91
21						$76.67	$1,869.20	$2,009.93	$2,161.24
22							$1,616.63	$1,738.33	$1,869.20
23							$1,398.18	$1,503.44	$1,616.63
24							$1,209.25	$1,300.29	$1,398.18
25							$1,045.85	$1,124.59	$1,209.25
26							$904.53	$972.63	$1,045.85
27							$782.31	$841.20	$904.53
28							$676.60	$727.53	$782.31
29							$585.17	$629.23	$676.60
30							$506.10	$544.20	$585.17
31							$437.71	$470.67	$506.10
32							$378.57	$407.07	$437.71
33							$327.41	$352.06	$378.57
34							$283.17	$304.49	$327.41
35							$244.91	$263.35	$283.17
36							$211.82	$227.76	$244.91

12.Put Option. Enter **0** in cell **B4**.

FIGURE 5. Spreadsheet Model of Binomial Option Pricing - Full-Scale Real Data - Put Option (Continued).

	A	B	C	D	E	F	AX	AY	AZ
1	**BINOMIAL OPTION PRICING**			**Full-Scale Real Data**					
2				**Put**	**Continuous**				
3	**Inputs**				**Outputs**				
4	Option Type: 1=Call, 0=Put	0		Time / Period		0.007			
5	Stock Price Now	$102.50		Riskfree Rate / Period		0.04%			
6	Standard Dev (Annual)	86.07%		Up Movement / Period		7.53%			
7	Riskfree Rate (Annual)	5.47%		Down Movement / Period		-7.00%			
8	Exercise Price	$100.00		Risk Neutral Probability		48.45%			
9	Time To Maturity (Years)	0.3556							
10	Number of Periods	50							
11	Annualization Convention: 1=Discrete, 0=Continuous	0							
12									
13		**Now**							**Maturity**
14	Period	0	1	2	3	4	48	49	50
15	Time	0.000	0.007	0.014	0.021	0.028	0.341	0.348	0.356
68									
69	Put	$18.18	$15.38	$12.79	$10.44	$8.35	$0.00	$0.00	$0.00
70			$20.83	$17.82	$15.01	$12.41	$0.00	$0.00	$0.00
71				$23.67	$20.49	$17.46	$0.00	$0.00	$0.00
72					$26.68	$23.35	$0.00	$0.00	$0.00
73						$29.84	$0.00	$0.00	$0.00
74							$0.00	$0.00	$0.00
75							$0.00	$0.00	$0.00
76							$0.00	$0.00	$0.00
77							$0.00	$0.00	$0.00
78							$0.00	$0.00	$0.00
79							$0.00	$0.00	$0.00
80							$0.00	$0.00	$0.00
81							$0.00	$0.00	$0.00
82							$0.00	$0.00	$0.00
83							$0.00	$0.00	$0.00
84							$0.00	$0.00	$0.00
85							$0.00	$0.00	$0.00
86							$0.00	$0.00	$0.00
87							$0.00	$0.00	$0.00
88							$0.00	$0.00	$0.00

We see that the Full-Scale Real Data model predicts an European put price of $18.18. This is only one cent different that what the Black-Scholes model predicts given identical inputs! The accuracy of the binomial model can be increased to any desired degree by increasing the number of periods. Whereas the Black Scholes model (and its natural extensions) is limited to a narrow range of derivatives, the Binomial Option Pricing model can be extended to price *any* derivative security (any type, any underlying asset(s), any underlying cash flows, any derivative payoffs).

[1] At full-scale (50 periods), the binomial option price is very insensitive to the expected return of the stock. For example, suppose that you calibrated this Amazon.com case to an annual expected return of 10%. Just add **10%*F4** to the formulas for the up and down movements / period. So the up movement / period in cell **F6** would become **=IF($B$11=1,10%*F4+B6*SQRT (F4),EXP(10%*F4+B6*SQRT(F4))-1)** and the down movement / period in cell **F7** would become **=IF($B$11=1, 10%*F4-B6*SQRT(F4), EXP(10%*F4-B6*SQRT(F4))-1)**. This changes the option price by less than 1/100th of one penny! In the (Black Scholes) limit as the number of (sub) periods goes to infinity, the option price becomes totally insensitive to the expected return of the stock. Because of this insensitivity, the conventions for calculating the up movement / period and down movement / period ignore the expected return of the stock.

BINOMIAL OPTION PRICING
Problems

Problems To Build And Use The Spreadsheet Models

1.The current stock price of a company is $37.50, the potential up movement / period of the stock price is 22.0%, the potential down movement / period of the stock price is -13.00%, the risk-free rate is 4.0% per period, the exercise price of an one-period, European call option on the stock is $39.00, the exercise price of an one-period, European put option on the stock is $39.00, the time to maturity for both options is 0.58 years, and the number of periods for both options is 1. Build the **Binomial Option Pricing - Single Period** model and use it to determine the current prices of the call and put.

2.The current stock price of a company is $23.75, the potential up movement / period of the stock price is 27.0%, the potential down movement / period of the stock price is -9.00%, the risk-free rate is 5.0% per period, the exercise price of an European call option on the stock is $22.00, the exercise price of an European put option on the stock is $22.00, the time to maturity for both options is 0.39 years, and the number of periods for both options is 8. Build the **Binomial Option Pricing - Multi-Period** model and use it to determine the current prices of the call and put.

3.The current stock price of a company is $43.25, the potential up movement / period of the stock price is 19.0%, the potential down movement / period of the stock price is -14.00%, the risk-free rate is 4.0% per period, the exercise price of an European call option on the stock is $45.00, the exercise price of an European put option on the stock is $45.00, the time to maturity for both options is 0.83 years, and the number of periods for both options is 8. Build the **Binomial Option Pricing - Risk Neutral** model and use it to determine the current prices of the call and put.

4.Collect Cisco Systems' historical stock prices from Yahoo Finance! From the financial media, collect the current stock price of Cisco Systems, the exercise price of an European call option on Cisco Systems, the exercise price of an European put option on Cisco Systems, the time to maturity for both options, and the yield on a risk-free Treasury Bill maturing as close as possible to the maturity date of the options. Build the **Binomial Option Pricing - Full-Scale Real Data** model and use it to determine:

• (a.) What is the annual standard deviation of Cisco Systems stock?

• (b.) What are the current prices of the call and put under the *continuous* annualization convention?

• (c.) What are the current prices of the call and put under the *discrete* annualization convention?

Problems To Extend The Spreadsheet Models.

5.Extend the **Binomial Option Pricing - Risk Neutral** model to incorporate a $2.00 / share dividend that will be paid out in period 5. In other words, all of the period 5 stock prices will be reduced by $2.00. Determine the current prices of the call and put.

6.Extend the **Binomial Option Pricing - Risk Neutral** model to analyze Digital Options. The only thing which needs to be changed is the option's payoff at maturity.

• (a.) For a Digital Call, the Payoff At Maturity = $1.00 When Stock Price At Maturity > Exercise Price Or $0.00 Otherwise.

• (b.) For a Digital Put, the Payoff At Maturity = $1.00 When Stock Price At Maturity < Exercise Price Or $0.00 Otherwise.

7.Extend the **Binomial Option Pricing - Full-Scale Real Data** model to determine how fast the binomial option price converges to the price in the **Black Scholes Option Pricing - Basics** model. Reduce the Full-Scale model to a 10 period model and to a 20 period model. Increase the 50 period model to a 100 period model. Then for the same inputs, compare call and put prices of the 10 period, 20 period, 50 period, 100 period, and Black-Scholes models.

8.Extend the **Binomial Option Pricing - Full-Scale Real Data** model to determine how fast the binomial option price with averaging of adjacent odd and even numbers of periods converges to the price in the **Black Scholes Option Pricing - Basics** model. As you increase the number of periods in the binomial model, it oscillates between overshooting and undershooting the true price. A simple technique to increase price efficiency is to average adjacent odd and even numbers of periods. For example, average the 10 period call price and the 11 period call price. Reduce the Full-Scale model to a 10 period, 11 period, 20 period, and 21 period model. Increase the 50 period model to a 51 period, 100 period, and 101 period model. Then for the same inputs, compare call and put prices of the average of the 10 and 11 period models, 20 and 21 period models, 50 and 51 period models, 100 and 101 period models, and Black-Scholes model.

BLACK SCHOLES OPTION PRICING
Basics

Problem. On December 13, 1999, the stock price of Amazon.com was $102.50, the continuous annual standard deviation was 86.07%, the yield on a risk-free Treasury Bill maturing on April 20th was 5.47%, the exercise price of an April 100 European call on Amazon.com was $100.00 the exercise price of an April 100 European put on Amazon.com was $100.00, and the time to maturity for both April 21st maturity options was 0.3556 years. What are the current prices of the call and put?   ,

FIGURE 1. Spreadsheet for Black Scholes Option Pricing - Basics.

	A	B	C	D	E	F
1	**BLACK SCHOLES OPTION PRICING**				**Basics**	
2						
3	**Inputs**					
4	Stock Price Now (P_s)	$102.50				
5	Standard Dev - Annual (σ)	86.07%				
6	Riskfree Rate - Annual (R)	5.47%				
7	Exercise Price (E)	$100.00				
8	Time To Maturity - Years (T)	0.3556				
9						
10	**Outputs**					
11	d1	0.343				
12	d2	-0.171				
13	N(d1)	0.634				
14	N(d2)	0.432				
15	Call Price (V_c)	$22.60				
16						
17	-d1	-0.343				
18	-d2	0.171				
19	N(-d1)	0.366				
20	N(-d2)	0.568				
21	Put Price (P_p)	$18.17				

How To Build This Spreadsheet Model.

1.Inputs. Enter the inputs described above into the range **B4:B8**.

2.d1 and d2 Formulas. The d_1 formula is:

$$\left(\ln\left(P_s / E\right) + \left(R + \sigma^2 / 2\right) \cdot T\right) / \left(\sigma \cdot \sqrt{T}\right)$$

In cell **B11**, enter **=(LN(B4/B7)+(B6+B5^2/2)*B8)/(B5*SQRT(B8))**

The d_2 formula is: $d_1 - \sigma\sqrt{T}$ In cell **B12**, enter **=B11-B5*SQRT(B8)**.

3.Cumulative Normal Formulas. Enter $N(d_1)$ using the cumulative normal function **NORMSDIST** in cell **B13 =NORMSDIST(B11)**

Copy the cell **B13** to cell **B14** or enter $N(d_2)$ using the cumulative normal function **NORMSDIST** in cell **B14 =NORMSDIST(B12)**

4.European Call Price Formula. The Black-Scholes call formula is:

$$V_c = P_s N(d_1) - Ee^{-RT} N(d_2)$$

In cell **B15**, enter **=B4*B13-B7*EXP(-B6*B8)*B14**

We see that the Black-Scholes model predicts an European call price of $22.60. This is only one cent different that what the Binominal Option Pricing - Full-Scale Real Data model predicts given identical inputs! Now let's do the put.

5.-d1 and -d2 Formulas. For the labels, enter **'-d1** in **A17** and **'-d2 A18**. The **'** tells Excel that it is a label, not a formula. For the two put formula terms, they are just opposite in sign from their call formula counterparts. Enter **=-B11** in **B17** and **=-B12** in **B18**.

6.Cumulative Normal Formulas. Enter $N(-d_1)$ using the cumulative normal function **NORMSDIST** in cell **B19 =NORMSDIST(B17)**

Copy the cell **B19** to cell **B20** or enter $N(-d_2)$ using the cumulative normal function **NORMSDIST** in cell **B20 =NORMSDIST(B18)**

7.European Put Price Formula. The Black-Scholes put formula is:

$$P_p = -P_s N(-d_1) + Ee^{-RT} N(-d_2)$$

In cell **B21**, enter **=-B4*B19+B7*EXP(-B6*B8)*B20**

We see that the Black-Scholes model predicts an European put price of $18.17. This is only one cent different that what the Binominal Option Pricing - Full-Scale Real Data model predicts given identical inputs! The advantage of the Black Scholes model (and its natural extensions) is that it is quick and easy to calculate, but the disadvantage is that it is limited to a narrow range of derivatives.

BLACK SCHOLES OPTION PRICING
Dynamic Chart

If you increased the standard deviation of the stock, what would happen to the price of the call option? If you increased the time to maturity, what would happen to the price of the call? You can answer these questions and more by creating an *Dynamic Chart* using "spinners." Spinners are up-arrow / down-arrow buttons that allow you to easily change the inputs to the model with the click of a mouse. Then the spreadsheet recalculates the model and instantly redraws the model outputs on the graph.

FIGURE 1. Spreadsheet model for Black Scholes Option Pricing - Dynamic Chart - Call Option.

How To Build This Spreadsheet Model.

1.Start with the Basics Spreadsheet, Rearrange the Rows, and Add A Switch. Open the spreadsheet that you created for Black Scholes Option Pricing - Basics and immediately save the spreadsheet under a new name using the **File Save As** command. Add six rows by selecting the range **A11:A16**, clicking on **Insert, Rows**. Select the range **A4:B4** and drag the range (hover the cursor over the lower highlighted line, click on the left mouse button, and hold it down while you move it) to cell **A13**. Enter **1** in cell **B4**. This will serve as a switch between a call option and a put option. To highlight which type of option is being graphed, enter **=IF($B$4=1,"Call","Put")** in cell **I1**.

2.Increase Row Height for the Spinners. Select the range **A4:A8**. Then click on **Format Row Height** from the main menu. Enter a height of **30** and click on **OK**.

3.Display the Forms Toolbar. Select **View Toolbars Forms** from the main menu.

4.Create the Spinners. Look for the up-arrow / down-arrow button on the **Forms** toolbar (which will display the word "Spinner" if you hover the cursor over it) and click on it. Then draw the box for a spinner from the upper left corner of cell **C4** down to the lower right corner of the cell. Then a spinner appears in the cell **C4**. Right click on the spinner (press the right mouse button while the cursor is above the spinner) and a small menu pops up. Click on **Copy**. Then select the cell **C5** and click on **Paste**. This creates an identical spinner in the cell **C5**. Repeat the process three times more. Select cell **C6** and click on **Paste**. Select cell **C7** and click on **Paste**. Select cell **C8** and click on **Paste**. You now have five spinners down column **C**.

5.Create The Cell Links. Right click on the first spinner in the cell **C4** and a small menu pops up. Click on **Format Control** and a dialog box pops up. Click on the **Control** tab, then enter the cell link **D4** in the **Cell link** edit box and click on OK. Repeat this procedure for the other four spinners. Link the spinner in cell **C5** to cell **D5**. Link the spinner in cell **C6** to cell **D6**. Link the spinner in cell **C7** to cell **D7**. Link the spinner in cell C8 to cell **D8**. Test your spinners by clicking on the up-arrows and down-arrows of the spinners to see how they change the values in the linked cells.

6.Create Scaled Inputs. The values in the linked cells are always integers, but they can be scaled appropriately to the problem at hand. Restrict the value in cell **B4** to be either 1 or 0 by entering **=IF(D4>1,1,D4)**. In cell **B5**, enter **=D5/10+0.001**. In cell **B6**, enter **=D6/100**. In cell **B7**, enter **=D7**. In cell **B8**, enter **=D8/10+0.001**. The additional terms **+0.001** in cells **B5** and **B8**, prevent the scaled value from going to zero when the linked cell goes to zero. When the standard deviation or a time to maturity literally became zero, then the Black Scholes call and put formulas blow-up.

7.Create Stock Price Inputs. In the range **B13:L13**, enter the values **0.01, 20, 40, 60, ..., 200**. In cell **M13**, enter **0.01**. In cell **N13**, enter **=B7**. In cell **O13**, enter **=L13**.

8.Convert The Input Cell References To Absolute References. In convert the input cell references contained in the formulas in cells **B17, B18, B21,** and **B27** to absolute references. That is, put $s in front of any references to the *input cells* in the range **B4:B8**. When you are done, the formula in cell **B17** will look like **= (LN(B13/$B$7)+($B$6+$B$5^2/2)*$B$8) / ($B$5*SQRT($B$8))**. Cell **B18** will look like **= B17-$B$5*SQRT($B$8)**. Cell **B21** will look like **=B13*B19-$B$7*EXP(-$B$6*$B$8)*B20**. Cell **B27** will look like **=-B13*B25+$B$7*EXP(-$B$6*$B$8)*B26**.

9.Copy The Formulas. Select the formulas in the range **B17:B27** and copy them to the range **C17:O27**.

10.Option Price. Reference the Call Price or the Put Price depending on which type of option is selected in cell **B4**. Enter **=IF($B$4=1,B21,B27)** in cell **B14** and copy the cell to the range **C14:L14**.

11.Add The Intrinsic Value. If the option was maturing now, rather than later, its payoff would be:

- For a call, **Max (Stock Price Now - Exercise Price, 0)**.

- For a put, **Max (Exercise Price - Stock Price Now, 0)**.

This is the so-called "Intrinsic Value" of the option. In cell **M15**, enter the formula **=IF (B4=1, MAX (M13-$B$7,0), MAX($B$7-M13,0))** and copy this cell to the range **N15:O15**.

12.Graph the Option Price and Intrinsic Value. Select the range **B13:O15**. Next choose **Insert Chart** from the main menu. Select an **XY(Scatter)** chart type and make other selections to complete the Chart Wizard. Place the graph in the range **E2:J11**.

FIGURE 2. Spreadsheet model for Black Scholes Option Pricing - Dynamic Chart - Put Option.

	A	B	C	D	E	F	G	H	I	J
1	**BLACK SCHOLES OPTION PRICING**				Dynamic Chart			Put		
2										
3	Inputs									
4	Option Type: 1=Call, 0=Put	0		0						
5	Standard Dev - Annual (σ)	90%		9						
6	Riskfree Rate - Annual (R)	6.0%		6						
7	Exercise Price (E)	$100.00		100						
8	Time To Maturity - Yrs (T)	0.40		4						
9										
10										
11										
12	Dynamic Chart Outputs									
13	Stock Price Now (P_s)	$0.01	$20.00	$40.00	$60.00	$80.00	$100.00	$120.00	$140.00	$160.00
14	Option Price	$97.61	$77.64	$58.50	$42.28	$29.92	$21.02	$14.78	$10.44	$7.43
15	Intrinsic Value									
16										
17	d1	-15.815	-2.493	-1.279	-0.568	-0.064	0.327	0.647	0.917	1.151
18	d2	-16.386	-3.064	-1.849	-1.138	-0.634	-0.243	0.076	0.347	0.581
19	N(d1)	0.000	0.006	0.101	0.285	0.475	0.628	0.741	0.820	0.875
20	N(d2)	0.000	0.001	0.032	0.127	0.263	0.404	0.530	0.636	0.719
21	Call Price (V_c)	$0.00	$0.02	$0.88	$4.66	$12.30	$23.40	$37.16	$52.82	$69.81
22										
23	-d1	15.815	2.493	1.279	0.568	0.064	-0.327	-0.647	-0.917	-1.151
24	-d2	16.386	3.064	1.849	1.138	0.634	0.243	-0.076	-0.347	-0.581
25	N(-d1)	1.000	0.994	0.899	0.715	0.525	0.372	0.259	0.180	0.125
26	N(-d2)	1.000	0.999	0.968	0.873	0.737	0.596	0.470	0.364	0.281
27	Put Price (P_p)	$97.61	$77.64	$58.50	$42.28	$29.92	$21.02	$14.78	$10.44	$7.43

Your *Dynamic Chart* allows you to change Black-Scholes inputs and instantly see the impact on a graph of the option price and intrinsic value. This allows you to perform instant experiments on the Black-Scholes option pricing model. Below is a list of experiments that you might want to perform:

- What happens when the standard deviation is increased?

- What happens when the time to maturity is increased?

- What happens when the exercise price is increased?

- What happens when the riskfree rate is increased?

- What happens when the dividend yield is increased?

- What happens when the standard deviation is really close to zero?

- What happens when the time to maturity is really close to zero?

Notice that the Black-Scholes option price is usually greater than the payoff you would obtain if the option was maturing today (the "intrinsic value"). This extra value is called the "Time Value" of the option. Given your result in the last experiment above, can you explain *why* the extra value is called the "Time Value"?

BLACK SCHOLES OPTION PRICING
Continuous Dividend

Problem. Amazon.com doesn't pay a dividend, but suppose that it did. Specifically, suppose that Amazon.com paid dividends in tiny amounts on a continuous basis throughout the year at a 3.00% / year rate. What would be the new price of the April 100 European call and April 100 European put?

Solution Strategy. Modify the Basics spreadsheet to incorporate the continuous dividend version of the Black Scholes model.

FIGURE 1. Spreadsheet for Black Scholes Option Pricing - Continuous Dividend.

	A	B	C	D	E	F	G	H
1	**BLACK SCHOLES OPTION PRICING**				**Continuous Dividend**			
2								
3	**Inputs**							
4	Stock Price Now (P_s)	$102.50						
5	Standard Dev - Annual (σ)	86.07%						
6	Riskfree Rate - Annual (R)	5.47%						
7	Exercise Price (E)	$100.00						
8	Time To Maturity - Years (T)	0.3556						
9	Dividend yield (d)	3.00%						
10								
11	**Outputs**							
12	d1	0.322						
13	d2	-0.191						
14	N(d1)	0.626						
15	N(d2)	0.424						
16	Call Price (V_c)	$21.91						
17								
18	-d1	-0.322						
19	-d2	0.191						
20	N(-d1)	0.374						
21	N(-d2)	0.576						
22	Put Price (P_p)	$18.57						

How To Build This Spreadsheet Model.

1.Start with the Basics Spreadsheet, Add A Row, and Enter The Dividend Yield. Open the spreadsheet that you created for Black Scholes Option Pricing - Basics and immediately save the spreadsheet under a new name using the **File Save As** command. Add a row by selecting the cell **A9** and clicking on **Insert Rows**. Enter the dividend yield in cell **A9**.

2.Modify the d1 Formula. In the continuous dividend version, the d_1 formula is modified by subtracting the continuous dividend yield d in the numerator. The new d_1 formula is:

$$\left(\ln\left(P_s / E\right) + \left(R - d + \sigma^2 / 2\right) \cdot T\right) / \left(\sigma \cdot \sqrt{T}\right)$$

In cell **B12**, enter **=(LN(B4/B7)+(B6-B9+B5^2/2)*B8)/(B5*SQRT(B8))**

3.Modify the Call Price Formula. The modified call formula is:

$$V_c = P_s e^{-dT} N\left(d_1\right) - E e^{-RT} N\left(d_2\right)$$

where d is the continuous dividend yield. In cell **B16**, enter**=B4*EXP(-B9*B8)*B14-B7*EXP(-B6*B8)*B15**

We see that the Black-Scholes Option Pricing - Continuous Dividend model predicts an European call price of $21.91. This is a drop of 69 cents from the no dividend version. Now let's do the put.

4.Modify the Put Price Formula. The modified put formula is :

$$P_p = -P_s e^{-dT} N\left(-d_1\right) + E e^{-RT} N\left(-d_2\right)$$

In cell **B22**, enter **=-B4*EXP(-B9*B8)*B20+B7*EXP (-B6*B8)*B21**

We see that the Black-Scholes model predicts an European put price of $18.57. This is a rise of 40 cents from the no dividend version.

BLACK SCHOLES OPTION PRICING
Implied Volatility

Problem. On December 14, 1999, the S&P 500 index closed at 1,403. European call and put options on the S&P 500 index with the exercise prices show below traded for the following prices:

Exercise price	1,350	1,375	1,400	1,425	1,450
Call price	$81	$66 1/4	$46	$31	$19 1/4
Put price	$18	$23 5/8	$30 1/2	$41 1/2	$55

These call options mature on January 21, 2000 (the third Friday of January). The S&P 500 portfolio pays a continuous dividend yield of 1.18% per year and the annual yield on a Treasury Bill which matures on January 20th is 5.34% per year. What is the implied volatility of each of these calls and puts? What pattern do these implied volatilities follow across exercise prices and between calls vs. puts?

Solution Strategy. Calculate the difference between the observed option price and the option price predicted by the continuous dividend yield version of the Black-Scholes model using a dummy value for the stock volatility. Have the Excel Solver tool adjust the stock volatility by trial and error until the difference between the observed price and the model price is equal to zero (within a very small error tolerance).

FIGURE 1. Spreadsheet for Black Scholes Option Pricing - Implied Volatility.

	A	B	C	D	E	F	G	H	I	J	K
1	**BLACK SCHOLES OPTION PRICING**					**Implied Volatility**					
2											
3	**Inputs**										
4	Option Type: 1=Call, 0=Put	1	1	1	1	1	0	0	0	0	0
5	Stock Price Now (P$_s$)	$1,403	$1,403	$1,403	$1,403	$1,403	$1,403	$1,403	$1,403	$1,403	$1,403
6	Riskfree Rate - Annual (R)	5.34%	5.34%	5.34%	5.34%	5.34%	5.34%	5.34%	5.34%	5.34%	5.34%
7	Exercise Price (E)	$1,350	$1,375	$1,400	$1,425	$1,450	$1,350	$1,375	$1,400	$1,425	$1,450
8	Time To Maturity - Yrs (T)	0.1028	0.1028	0.1028	0.1028	0.1028	0.1028	0.1028	0.1028	0.1028	0.1028
9	Dividend yield (d)	1.18%	1.18%	1.18%	1.18%	1.18%	1.18%	1.18%	1.18%	1.18%	1.18%
10	Observed Option Price	$81.00	$66.25	$46.00	$31.00	$19.25	$18.00	$23.63	$30.50	$41.50	$55.00
11											
12	**Outputs**										
13	d1	0.556	0.329	0.125	-0.129	-0.419	0.612	0.389	0.136	-0.161	-0.504
14	d2	0.472	0.244	0.051	-0.198	-0.482	0.537	0.320	0.073	-0.219	-0.558
15	N(d1)	0.711	0.629	0.550	0.448	0.338	0.730	0.651	0.554	0.436	0.307
16	N(d2)	0.682	0.596	0.520	0.422	0.315	0.704	0.625	0.529	0.413	0.288
17	Model Call Price (V$_c$)	$81.00	$66.25	$46.00	$31.00	$19.25	$76.86	$57.62	$39.63	$25.77	$14.41
18											
19	-d1	-0.556	-0.329	-0.125	0.129	0.419	-0.612	-0.389	-0.136	0.161	0.504
20	-d2	-0.472	-0.244	-0.051	0.198	0.482	-0.537	-0.320	-0.073	0.219	0.558
21	N(-d1)	0.289	0.371	0.450	0.552	0.662	0.270	0.349	0.446	0.564	0.693
22	N(-d2)	0.318	0.404	0.480	0.578	0.685	0.296	0.375	0.471	0.587	0.712
23	Model Put Price (P$_p$)	$22.14	$32.25	$36.87	$46.73	$59.84	$18.00	$23.62	$30.50	$41.50	$55.00
24											
25	**Solver**										
26	Differ (observed - model)	4E-07	3E-08	9E-07	2E-08	1E-07	7E-08	7E-08	1E-08	8E-07	1E-07
27	Implied Volatility from Calls	26.03%	26.73%	23.11%	21.28%	19.78%					
28	Implied Volatility from Puts						23.30%	21.60%	19.52%	18.33%	16.78%

How To Build This Spreadsheet Model.

1.Start with the Continuous Dividend Spreadsheet, Rearrange The Rows, and Add A Switch. Open the spreadsheet that you created for Black Scholes Option Pricing - Continuous Dividend and immediately save the spreadsheet under a new name using the **File Save As** command. Add a row by selecting the cell **A4** and clicking on **Insert Rows**. Select the range **A6:B6** and drag the range (hover the cursor over the lower highlighted line, click on the left mouse button, and hold it down while you move it) to cell **A27**. Select the range **A7:B10** and drag the range to cell **A6**. Enter **1** in cell **B4**. This will serve as a switch between a call option and a put option.

2.Enter the January 1,350 Call Inputs. Enter the inputs for the January 1,350 Call in the range **B4:B9** and enter the observed option price for the January 1,350 Call the in cell **B10**.

3.Difference (Observed - Model). The Difference (Observed - Model) is:

- Observed Option Price - Model Call Price for a Call Option

- Observed Option Price - Model Put Price for a Put Option.

Enter **=IF(B4=1,B10-B17,B10-B23)**in cell **B26**.

4.Copy the Entire Column over Nine More Columns. Select the range **B4:B27** and copy it to the range **C4:K27**.

5.Enter the Options Inputs. In the range **B4:F2**, enter the inputs for the five call options. In the range **G4:K27**, enter the inputs for the five put options. Select the put volatilities in the range **G27:K27** and drag the range down to cell **G28**.

6.Call Up Excel Solver. From Excel's main menu, click on **Tools** and then Solver. If you don't see **Solver** on the **Tools** Menu, then click on **Tools Add-Ins**, check the **Solver Add-In** box, and click on **OK**.)

7.Set-up Solver. In the Solver dialog box, enter cell **B26** as the <u>Set Target Cell</u>. In the <u>Equal to</u> row, click on the option button for <u>Value of</u> and enter **0** in the adjacent box. Enter cell **B27** as the <u>By Changing Cell</u>. See figure below.

FIGURE 2. Solver dialog box.

8.Run Solver. Click on the Solve button.

By trial and error, the Solver adjusts the value of the Implied Volatility in cell **B27** until the Difference (Observed - Model) in cell **B26** equals zero (within a very small error tolerance). This results in an implied volatility of 26.03%. Your results may differ by a slight amount (usually only in the second decimal) depending on Solver's error tolerance.

9.Repeat. Repeat steps **7** and **8** to solve the problems in columns **D, E, ..., K**.

10.Graph the Implied Volatilities Across Exercise Prices and Option Types. Highlight the range **B7:K7**, then hold down the Control button and (while still holding it down) select the range **B27:K28**. Next choose **Insert Chart** from the main menu. Select an **XY(Scatter)** chart type and make other selections to complete the Chart Wizard.

FIGURE 3. Graph of the "Scowl" Pattern of Implied Volatilities.

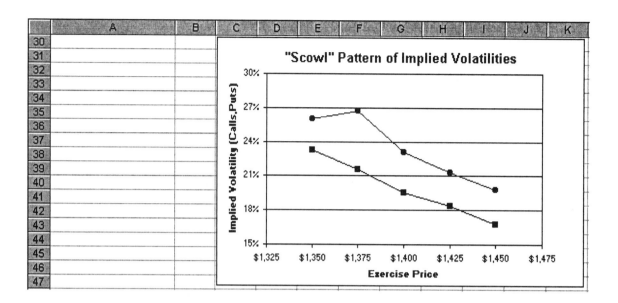

If the market's beliefs about the distribution of returns of the S&P 500 Index matched the theoretical distribution of returns assumed by the Black-Scholes model, then all of the implied volatilities would be the same. From the graph we see this is not the case. The implied volatility pattern declines sharply with the exercise price and puts have lower implied volatilities than calls. In the '70s and '80s, the typical implied volatility pattern was a U-shaped, "Smile" pattern. Since the '90s, it is more typical to see a downward-sloping, "Scowl" pattern.

BLACK SCHOLES OPTION PRICING
Problems

Problems To Build And Use The Spreadsheet Models

1.The current stock price of a company is $54.50, the continuous annual standard deviation was 53.00%, the exercise price of an European call on the stock is $58.00, the exercise price of an European put on the stock is $58.00, the time to maturity for both options is 0.43 years, and the yield on a risk-free Treasury Bill maturing on the same date at the options is 6.72%. Build the **Black Scholes Option Pricing - Basics** model and use it to determine the current prices of the call and put.

2.Build the **Black Scholes Option Pricing - Dynamic Chart** model and use it to perform instant experiments on whether changing various inputs causes an increase or decrease in the Call Price and in the Put Price and by how much.

(a.) What happens when the standard deviation is increased?

(b.) What happens when the time to maturity is increased?

(c.) What happens when the exercise price is increased?

(d.) What happens when the riskfree rate is increased?

(e.) What happens when the dividend yield is increased?

(f.) What happens when the standard deviation is really close to zero?

(g.) What happens when the time to maturity is really close to zero?

3.The current stock price of a company is $39.25, the continuous annual standard deviation was 47.00%, the exercise price of an European call on the stock is $36.00, the exercise price of an European put on the stock is $36.00, the time to maturity for both options is 0.82 years, the yield on a risk-free Treasury Bill maturing on the same date at the options is 4.23%, and the continuous dividend paid throughout the year at the rate of 2.40% / year rate. Build the **Black Scholes Option Pricing - Contin**. Dividend model and use it to determine the current prices of the call and put.

4.The S&P 500 index closes at 2000. European call and put options on the S&P 500 index with the exercise prices show below trade for the following prices:

Exercise price	1,950	1,975	2,000	2,025	2,050
Call price	$88	$66	$47	$33	$21
Put price	$25	$26	$32	$44	$58

All options mature in 88 days. The S&P 500 portfolio pays a continuous dividend yield of 1.56% per year and the annual yield on a Treasury Bill which matures on the same day as the options is 4.63% per year. Build the **Black Scholes Option Pricing - Implied Volatility** model and use it to determine what is the implied volatility of each of these calls and puts. What pattern do these implied volatilities follow across exercise prices and between calls vs. puts?

SPOT-FUTURES PARITY (COST OF CARRY)
Basics

Problem. Suppose we recorded the monthly spot price of the S&P 500 index and corresponding futures price over a seven month period for a stock index futures contract maturing in month 7. Here are the prices in index points:

Month	1	2	3	4	5	6	7
Spot price	1117.36	1126.37	1136.73	1146.86	1155.14	1165.69	1178.23
Futures price	1144.38	1149.94	1155.05	1162.00	1167.24	1170.23	1178.23

Suppose that the riskfree rate is 0.42% per month. Analyze what happened over time to the basis and to the price difference between the model futures price implied by Spot-Futures Parity versus the actual futures price.

Solution Strategy. First calculate the basis. Then substitute the spot price into the Spot-Futures Parity to determine the model futures price. Then calculate the price difference between the model futures price and the actual futures price.

FIGURE 1. Spreadsheet for Spot-Future Parity (Cost of Carry) - Basics.

How To Build This Spreadsheet Model.

1.Inputs. Enter the inputs into the range **B4:H7**.

2.Basis (Futures - Spot). The formula for the Basis = Futures Price - Spot Price. Enter **=B6-B5** in cell **B10** and copy the cell to the range **C10:H10**

3.Time To Maturity (months). In month t, the formula for Time To Maturity(t) = Maturity Date - Current Date(t). Enter **=$H$4-B4** in cell **B11** and copy the cell to the range **C11:H11**. The $s lock in the maturity date.

4.Model Futures Price. The Spot-Futures Parity formula predicts the Futures Price = Spot Price * (1 + Riskfree Rate) ^(Time to Maturity). Enter **=B5*(1+B7)^B11** in cell **B12** and copy the cell to the range **C12:H12**.

5.Price Difference (Model - Observed). The price difference = model futures price - actual futures price. Enter **=B12-B6** in cell **B13** and copy the cell to the range **C13:H13**.

6.Graph the Futures and Spot Prices Over Time. Highlight the range **B4:H6**, then hold down the Control button and (while still holding it down) select the range **B12:H12**. Next choose **Insert Chart** from the main menu. Select an **XY(Scatter)** chart type and make other selections to complete the Chart Wizard.

Notice that the basis is a substantial positive value and steadily declines over time before finally reaching zero when the futures contract matures. By contrast, the price difference is very small value and fluctuates between positive and negative values before going to zero when the futures contract matures.

SPOT-FUTURES PARITY (COST OF CARRY)
Index Arbitrage

Given that there is a (nonzero) price difference between the two markets, is it possible to make an arbitrage profit? Suppose that the round trip transaction cost for doing an index arbitrage trade is 1.60 index points. Analyze the monthly data to determine if was possible to have made an arbitrage profit.

FIGURE 1. Spreadsheet for Spot-Future Parity (Cost of Carry) - Index Arbitrage.

	A	B	C	D	E	F	G	H
1	**SPOT-FUTURES PARITY (COST OF CARRY)**					**Index Arbitrage**		
2								
3	**Inputs**							**Maturity**
4	Calendar Time (months)	1	2	3	4	5	6	7
5	Observed Spot Price	1,417.8	1,436.3	1,426.6	1,456.8	1,455.5	1,460.2	1,476.6
6	Observed Futures Price	1,452.7	1,467.9	1,451.4	1,472.8	1,466.7	1,467.1	1,476.6
7	Risk-free rate / month	0.42%	0.42%	0.42%	0.42%	0.42%	0.42%	0.42%
8								
9	**Outputs**							
10	Basis (Futures - Spot)	34.9	31.6	24.8	16.0	11.2	6.9	0.0
11	Time to Maturity (months)	6	5	4	3	2	1	0
12	Model Futures Price	1,453.9	1,466.7	1,450.7	1,475.2	1,467.8	1,466.3	1,476.6
13	Price Difference (model-observed)	1.2	(1.2)	(0.7)	2.4	1.1	(0.8)	0.0
14	Transaction Costs (upper bound)	1.6	1.6	1.6	1.6	1.6	1.6	1.6
15	Transaction Costs (lower bound)	(1.6)	(1.6)	(1.6)	(1.6)	(1.6)	(1.6)	(1.6)
16								

How To Build This Spreadsheet Model.

1. Start with the Basics Spreadsheet. Open the spreadsheet that you created for Spot-Futures Parity (Cost of Carry) - Basics and immediately save the spreadsheet under a new name using the **File Save As** command. Delete the Futures and Spot Prices graph by clicking on it and pressing the **Delete** button.

2.Transaction Cost Bounds. Transaction costs create an upper bound and a lower bound on the price difference, within which it is not possible to make an arbitrage profit. Specify the upper bound by entering **1.60** in cell **B14** and the lower bound by entering **-1.60** in cell **B15**. Copy the range **B14:B15** to the range **C14:H15**.

3.Graph the Price Difference and Transaction Costs. Highlight the range **B4:H4**, then hold down the Control button and (while still holding it down) select the range **B13:H15**. Next choose **Insert Chart** from the main menu. Select an **XY(Scatter)** chart type and make other selections to complete the Chart Wizard.

Most of the time the price difference was inside the transaction cost boundaries, so there was not an arbitrage opportunity. However in month 4, the price difference went outside the boundaries by rising above the upper bound. Thus, an arbitrage profit could made in month 4 by selling in the index portfolio in the spot market, using the proceeds to lend money at the riskfree rate, and going long in the futures market.

SPOT-FUTURES PARITY (COST OF CARRY)
Problems

Problems To Build And Use The Spreadsheet Models

1. Suppose we recorded the monthly spot price of the S&P 500 index and corresponding futures price over a seven month period for a stock index futures contract maturing in month 7. Here are the prices in index points:

Month	1	2	3	4	5	6	7
Spot price	1539.21	1552.95	1587.44	1603.48	1659.12	1653.47	1693.59
Futures price	1590.33	1593.68	1619.93	1630.37	1679.38	1679.38	1693.59

Suppose that the riskfree rate is 0.53% per month. Build the **Spot-Futures Parity (Cost Of Carry) - Basics** model and use it to analyze what happened over time to the basis and to the price difference between the model futures price implied by Spot-Futures Parity versus the actual futures price.

2. The round trip transaction cost for doing an index arbitrage trade is 1.60 index points. Build the **Spot-Futures Parity (Cost Of Carry) - Index Arbitrage** model and use it to analyze the monthly data above to determine if was possible to have made an arbitrage profit.

SINGLE PC LICENSE AGREEMENT AND LIMITED WARRANTY

READ THIS LICENSE CAREFULLY BEFORE USING THIS PACKAGE. BY USING THIS PACKAGE, YOU ARE AGREEING TO THE TERMS AND CONDITIONS OF THIS LICENSE. IF YOU DO NOT AGREE, DO NOT OPEN THE PACKAGE. PROMPTLY RETURN THE UNOPENED PACKAGE AND ALL ACCOMPANYING ITEMS TO THE PLACE YOU OBTAINED THEM [[FOR A FULL REFUND OF ANY SUMS YOU HAVE PAID FOR THE SOFTWARE]]. *THESE TERMS APPLY TO ALL LICENSED SOFTWARE ON THE DISK EXCEPT THAT THE TERMS FOR USE OF ANY SHAREWARE OR FREEWARE ON THE DISKETTES ARE AS SET FORTH IN THE ELECTRONIC LICENSE LOCATED ON THE DISK:*

1. GRANT OF LICENSE and OWNERSHIP: The enclosed computer programs <<and data>> ("Software") are licensed, not sold, to you by Prentice-Hall, Inc. ("We" or the "Company") and in consideration [[of your payment of the license fee, which is part of the price you paid]] [[of your purchase or adoption of the accompanying Company textbooks and/or other materials,]] and your agreement to these terms. We reserve any rights not granted to you. You own only the disk(s) but we and/or our licensors own the Software itself. This license allows you to use and display your copy of the Software on a single computer (i.e., with a single CPU) at a single location for <u>academic</u> use only, so long as you comply with the terms of this Agreement. You may make one copy for back up, or transfer your copy to another CPU, provided that the Software is usable on only one computer.

2. RESTRICTIONS: You may <u>not</u> transfer or distribute the Software or documentation to anyone else. Except for backup, you may <u>not</u> copy the documentation or the Software. You may <u>not</u> network the Software or otherwise use it on more than one computer or computer terminal at the same time. You may <u>not</u> reverse engineer, disassemble, decompile, modify, adapt, translate, or create derivative works based on the Software or the Documentation. You may be held legally responsible for any copying or copyright infringement which is caused by your failure to abide by the terms of these restrictions.

3. TERMINATION: This license is effective until terminated. This license will terminate automatically without notice from the Company if you fail to comply with any provisions or limitations of this license. Upon termination, you shall destroy the Documentation and all copies of the Software. All provisions of this Agreement as to limitation and disclaimer of warranties, limitation of liability, remedies or damages, and our ownership rights shall survive termination.

4. LIMITED WARRANTY AND DISCLAIMER OF WARRANTY: Company warrants that for a period of 60 days from the date you purchase this SOFTWARE (or purchase or adopt the accompanying textbook), the Software, when properly installed and used in accordance with the Documentation, will operate in substantial conformity with the description of the Software set forth in the Documentation, and that for a period of 30 days the disk(s) on which the Software is delivered shall be free from defects in materials and workmanship under normal use. The Company does <u>not</u> warrant that the Software will meet your requirements or that the operation of the Software will be uninterrupted or error-free. Your only remedy and the Company's only obligation under these limited warranties is, at the Company's option, return of the disk for a refund of any amounts paid for it by you or replacement of the disk. THIS LIMITED WARRANTY IS THE ONLY WARRANTY PROVIDED BY THE COMPANY AND ITS LICENSORS, AND THE COMPANY AND ITS LICENSORS DISCLAIM ALL OTHER WARRANTIES, EXPRESS OR IMPLIED, INCLUDING WITHOUT LIMITATION, THE IMPLIED WARRANTIES OF MERCHANTABILITY AND FITNESS FOR A PARTICULAR PURPOSE. THE COMPANY DOES NOT WARRANT, GUARANTEE OR MAKE ANY REPRESENTATION REGARDING THE ACCURACY, RELIABILITY, CURRENTNESS, USE, OR RESULTS OF USE, OF THE SOFTWARE.

5. LIMITATION OF REMEDIES AND DAMAGES: IN NO EVENT, SHALL THE COMPANY OR ITS EMPLOYEES, AGENTS, LICENSORS, OR CONTRACTORS BE LIABLE FOR ANY INCIDENTAL, INDIRECT, SPECIAL, OR CONSEQUENTIAL DAMAGES ARISING OUT OF OR IN CONNECTION WITH THIS LICENSE OR THE SOFTWARE, INCLUDING FOR LOSS OF USE, LOSS OF DATA, LOSS OF INCOME OR PROFIT, OR OTHER LOSSES, SUSTAINED AS A RESULT OF INJURY TO ANY PERSON, OR LOSS OF OR DAMAGE TO PROPERTY, OR CLAIMS OF THIRD PARTIES, EVEN IF THE COMPANY OR AN AUTHORIZED REPRESENTATIVE OF THE COMPANY HAS BEEN ADVISED OF THE POSSIBILITY OF SUCH DAMAGES. IN NO EVENT SHALL THE LIABILITY OF THE COMPANY FOR DAMAGES WITH RESPECT TO THE SOFTWARE EXCEED THE AMOUNTS ACTUALLY PAID BY YOU, IF ANY, FOR THE SOFTWARE OR THE ACCOMPANYING TEXTBOOK. BECAUSE SOME

JURISDICTIONS DO NOT ALLOW THE LIMITATION OF LIABILITY IN CERTAIN CIRCUMSTANCES, THE ABOVE LIMITATIONS MAY NOT ALWAYS APPLY TO YOU.

6. GENERAL: THIS AGREEMENT SHALL BE CONSTRUED IN ACCORDANCE WITH THE LAWS OF THE UNITED STATES OF AMERICA AND THE STATE OF NEW YORK, APPLICABLE TO CONTRACTS MADE IN NEW YORK, AND SHALL BENEFIT THE COMPANY, ITS AFFILIATES AND ASSIGNEES. HIS AGREEMENT IS THE COMPLETE AND EXCLUSIVE STATEMENT OF THE AGREEMENT BETWEEN YOU AND THE COMPANY AND SUPERSEDES ALL PROPOSALS OR PRIOR AGREEMENTS, ORAL, OR WRITTEN, AND ANY OTHER COMMUNICATIONS BETWEEN YOU AND THE COMPANY OR ANY REPRESENTATIVE OF THE COMPANY RELATING TO THE SUBJECT MATTER OF THIS AGREEMENT. If you are a U.S. Government user, this Software is licensed with "restricted rights" as set forth in subparagraphs (a)-(d) of the Commercial Computer-Restricted Rights clause at FAR 52.227-19 or in subparagraphs (c)(1)(ii) of the Rights in Technical Data and Computer Software clause at DFARS 252.227-7013, and similar clauses, as applicable.

Should you have any questions concerning this agreement or if you wish to contact the Company for any reason, please contact in writing: [Faculty Services, Prentice Hall, One Lake Street, Upper Saddle River, NJ 07458